The Parisian Prowler

# THE
# PARISIAN
# PROWLER

*Le Spleen de Paris*

*Petits Poèmes en prose*

SECOND EDITION

by

Charles Baudelaire

TRANSLATED BY EDWARD K. KAPLAN

THE UNIVERSITY OF GEORGIA PRESS

Athens and London

I want to thank Arundhati Banerjee, Wallace Fowlie, Stephen Gendzier, Richard Howard, and Harry Zohn for their generous readings and suggestions. To Janna, Jeremy, Aaron, and Sima Kaplan I express my love.
This second edition has benefitted from the criticism and support of Ryszard Engelking, Rosemary Lloyd, Laurence M. Porter, Graham Robb, Marilyn Gaddis Rose, and my students.

Published by the University of Georgia Press
Athens, Georgia 30602
© 1989, 1997 by Edward K. Kaplan

Designed by Louise OFarrell
Set in 11/13 Bodoni Book
The paper in this book meets the guidelines for permanence and durability of the Committee on Production guidelines for Book Longevity of the Council on Library Resources.

Printed in the United States of America
01 00          P 5 4 3 2

Library of Congress Cataloging in Publication Data
Baudelaire, Charles, 1821–1867.
[Spleen de Paris. English]
The Parisian prowler : Le spleen de Paris, petits poèmes en prose, second edition / Charles Baudelaire ; Edward K. Kaplan, trans.
p.  cm.
Includes bibliographical references.
ISBN 0-8203-1879-5 (pbk. : alk. paper)
1. Prose poems, French—Translations into English.   2. Paris (France)—Poetry.   I. Kaplan, Edward K., 1942– .   II. Title.
PQ2191.S6E5   1997
841′.8—DC20          96–32135

British Library Cataloging in Publication Data available

# CONTENTS

# PREFACE

My original introduction was brief, only hinting at an interpretation developed at length in my book, *Baudelaire's Prose Poems: The Esthetic, the Ethical, and the Religious in "The Parisian Prowler"* (University of Georgia Press, 1990). Now the success of *The Parisian Prowler*, an American translation of Baudelaire's no-longer "neglected masterpiece," calls for a second, and improved, edition. I have corrected some errors and infelicities in the text as I strive to remain faithful to the French source, suggesting its tones and ambiguities as well as translating the lexicon. The illustrations I chose remain the same, for they constitute in their own right a graphic subtext to my version of *Le Spleen de Paris*, gradually unveiling the positive values beneath the narrator's often cruel, cynical, seductive, or hedonistic moods.

## AN ETHICAL BAUDELAIRE

Baudelaire is first and foremost an ironist who eschews what he calls the "heresy of didacticism." To avoid piloting his audience like Victor Hugo, he created a new, often puzzling genre that he provisionally labeled as "prose poems." Since most of the pieces are short narratives, I prefer to call them postromantic parables or paradoxical fables—whose meanings are not spelled out. They defy our stereotypes and wishful thinking for the purpose of engaging readers in dialogue. Baudelaire assumes his readers to be "hypocritical" (as he said at the opening of *Les Fleurs du Mal*)—deceptive, but also prone to self-deception. Truth is the fulcrum.

Baudelaire forces us to respond, to examine ourselves, and to scrutinize the narrator. We remain vigilant. What I call "ethical irony" is the key to penetrating his poses and disguises: moral insensitivity, anger, or even crude misogyny should arouse self-reflection. (Baudelaire parodies this Socratic method in the grotesquely comic story "Let's Beat Up the Poor!") Beneath his alienation, the narrator proves to be attuned to his human environment.

Indirectly for the most part, but not always, he affirms the preciousness of friendship and love—and community—despite repeated evidence that he will forever remain apart. While castigating naive optimism, he asserts the reality principle and, less obviously, forms models of human kindness. The Parisian Prowler is an impecunious urban writer and a lonely, compassionate man who yearns for affection.

The illustrations highlight these less obvious aspects of Baudelaire's "modern and more abstract" mind (see appendix, letter to his editor Arsène Houssaye). The art that accompanies the text disputes, gently but deliberately, the received view of the narrator as militant esthete, a solitary dandy who values only imaginative stimulation.

At the outset, two portraits introduce the author as our companion. The cover displays an etching by Alfred Briend of a Baudelaire self-portrait, purportedly inspired by hashish. At first I hesitated to promote this familiar legend of the "poet of evil," sinister and hallucinating, since his ethical irony undermines it. Yet the "legend" is not entirely false. Baudelaire's contradictory, eccentric personality does unify all fifty pieces of *The Parisian Prowler.*

The frontispiece—a photographic portrait of Baudelaire by Carjat—is emblematic of the collection as a whole. Dated 1863, during the period that he wrote most of the prose poems, *Baudelaire at the Etchings* depicts a connoisseur of art, consecrating the work's modernity in the transitional "age of mechanical reproduction" of Walter Benjamin's insightful phrase. And the author was about forty years of age—like several of his characters: the impoverished father in "The Eyes of the Poor," the disenchanted bachelors in "Portraits of Mistresses," and the narrator of "Miss Scalpel." Here he appears as he was: an elegant poet, art critic, and essayist who views us with equivocal approval, disdain, or distance.

The photograph's artistic décor also suggests that *The Parisian Prowler* is a multimedia undertaking, composed of words, people, and pictures, and a translation from one idiom to another. On Baudelaire's right (our left) we see a contemporary fashion vignette, and on his left a caricature of a bourgeois in a top hat. Similar individuals populate the book.

Inside, two drawings by Baudelaire reinforce this feeling of intimacy with the author. A sensuous sketch of Jeanne Duval, his mulatta mistress, accompanies "Beautiful Dorothy," another avatar of the "black Venus" poems in *Les Fleurs du Mal*. The caricature alongside "The Counterfeit Coin" pokes fun at the author's chronic insecurities—financial and professional—and his vulnerable self-esteem. Dreams of cash, as well as publicity, obsessed the writer, as summarized in "The Temptations, or Eros, Plutus, and Fame." Yet these narratives are fictions, not confessions.

Attentive readers enter Baudelaire's subtle fables more fully through their pensive, humane quality. Selected works by Édouard Manet and James McNeill Whistler—one French and the other American—provide the graphic backbone of an ethical reading. My choice of their work is both personal and deliberate. Baudelaire knew Manet, who, like himself, invented a controversial style of artistic realism, and he admired Whistler's art. And it seemed appropriate for Whistler's work to accompany the translator's, a New Englander also inspired by Paris. We are among friends.

Manet's *The Philosopher* and Whistler's *La Mère Gérard* (both of them evoking Paris of the 1860s) introduce the two brief, prosaic parables, "The Stranger" and "The Old Woman's Despair," which define the collection's generative theme:

love of family, friendship, nation, beauty, money, and God (and, dialectically, the narrator's ambivalent contempt for these very values). A man and a woman introduce his two opposing drives: the broadly defined "esthetic" (living within mind or imagination) versus the "ethical" (seeking real human contact).

Manet's "philosopher" (the title itself is ironic) appears as a miserable vagrant whose sad eyes avoid us, conveying his inability to relate to another person. This "enigmatic man"— as the narrator calls him—is an *esthetic stranger* who eludes social responsibility through fantasy, literally getting high on clouds. The rebuffed heroine of the second piece is the collection's *ethical stranger.* Accordingly, Whistler's Parisian bag lady stares at us with a crazed and fearful look, evoking her frustrated wishes for affection or reciprocated love. Fables like "The Old Acrobat," in fact, also deplore an old person's solitude and even childlessness.

Manet's other etchings continue to undermine the narrator's sometimes ruthless estheticism, his quest for exquisite sensations (or beauty). *Child Carrying a Tray* accompanies the horrifying parable of art and exploitation, "The Rope," in which a boy commits suicide, probably depressed by his parents' neglect and by the painter's insensitivity (only implied by the narrator). Baudelaire's dedication of the fable to Manet indeed suggests that the artist himself had sacrificed the needy child to his professional passion. Similar conflicts between ethical and esthetic values are repeated in "A Joker," "Crowds," "The Old Acrobat," and "The Cake." Manet's *Le Chanteur Espagnol,* which accompanies "Vocations," features that fable's fourth boy, the *misunderstood* one, who, like the author, remains unable to escape from his native land, as oppressive as it may feel.

Central to this edition is Manet's *The Absinthe Drinker,* an ironic counterpoint to "Get High," Baudelaire's famed esthetic manifesto: "So as not to be the martyred slaves of Time, get high; get high constantly! On wine, on poetry, or on virtue, as you wish." Yet a careful reading of this famous fable (previously known as "Get Drunk") reveals that hymn to intoxication to be misleading. Manet's alcoholic (who wears a top hat like Baudelaire) and his discarded bottle announce a contradictory message: such an "artificial paradise" is both compelling and temporary.

This picture and Manet's *The Philosopher* (also showing a scrap vessel at bottom right) echo the crass parable of failed inspiration, "The Wild Woman and the Affected Coquette," which ends: "and if you irk me too often with your *precious* whinings, I'll treat you like a *wild woman,* or I'll throw you out the window, like an empty bottle." Here, the poet/narrator blames a female muse or lover (as he often does) for the hollow flask of his own inspiration. However, in light of the author's ethical irony, "Get High" reminds us, almost subliminally, that fantasy cannot solidify our position in the world.

Whistler's four pictures maintain a corresponding ethical realism, starting with *La Mère Gérard.* Accompanying the touching fable "Widows," Whistler's *Finette*—a renowned French actress dressed in black like Baudelaire's majestic heroine—turns her eyes thoughtfully, peacefully, inward; her isolation as well is symbolized by an empty container, while a window opens onto a balcony and a city landscape, that of Paris, in the distance. Baudelaire's "Widows" ends poetically, as the narrator celebrates the pensive, lonely mother with blank verse—impossible to translate adequately. This poetry of bereavement sustains a woman in her own right, a fertile, loving mother—but, like the Prowler, afflicted, essentially alone.

Fantasy also provides opportunities to create. Whistler's *Rotherhithe,* placed between "A Hemisphere in Tresses" and "Invitation to the Voyage"—the collection's rare verselike prose—sensibly localizes Baudelaire's imaginative voyages. Dutch merchants sit, immobile, sharing pipe dreams, commercial or otherwise. Their relaxed ruminations are framed by ships' intricate rigging, anticipating the brief, but significant transitional piece, "The Harbor." Whistler's dreamers suggest how writing poetry may crystallize "enriched thoughts returning from the Infinite toward you," the beloved.

Later in the collection such utopias collapse. "The Soup and the Clouds" brutally parodies similar reveries: a literal-minded woman reduces the poet to what he actually is: "A goddamn cloud peddlar." Baudelaire is resolutely *post*romantic: the poet is an incurable idealist now demystified— as in "Loss of Halo"—by his dependence upon obtuse and tasteless consumers. He has subverted his professed religion of art and imagination, definitively.

Other fables reiterate Baudelaire's essential "question of reality." The final Whistler etching in this collection, a sad, dark image to which he also gave a French title, *La Vieille aux loques* (the old woman in rags), illustrates "Windows" directly and without irony. This parable of the literary art claims, rhetorically, that fantasy produces more light, and more life, than direct communication with another person. Speaking as a *writer* he asks: "Does it matter what the reality located outside of me might be, if it has helped me to live, to feel that I am and *what* I am?" After all, his "legends" do elicit tears of compassion. But *readers* still wonder: Is interpersonal reality truly irrelevant? While Baudelaire appears to justify fiction above truth, the question persists. We increasingly suspect that solipsism is not the way.

Our interpretation might boil down to an ethical dilemma: Would the esthete really trade "an eternity of damnation" in order to experience for just "*one* second the infinity of delight?" ("The Bad Glazier"). Does the writer who gazes from the outside through windows, open or closed, really care if his projections are true or false? ("Windows"). These sophisticated parables of creativity ponder the unseizable logic of literature.

Pictures by Honoré Daumier, whom Baudelaire admired as a social painter, detail the narrator's genuine compassion as well as his ironic self-criticism. *The Saltimbanques Changing Place* illustrates "The Old Acrobat," a poignant allegory of an obsolete intellectual. Daumier's family of wandering entertainers—consisting of mother, father, and boy—silhouettes the stroller's own frustrated longings for a stable and complete household. Baudelaire's buffoon represents "the old poet without friends, without family, without children, debased by his wretchedness and the public's ingratitude." He is an irremediable bachelor, unhappy, like Franz Kafka's "Fasting Artist," paradoxically refusing nourishment in order to earn a spiritual gift he can never receive.

Daumier's paintings also depict a philosophy of creativity. *Connoisseurs—Les Amateurs de peintures* reminds us that "Plans," which it illustrates, consists of fantasies derived, not from life, but from yet another art form. The anonymous observers, again with top hats, inspect the details, suggesting that readers, too, should scrutinize Baudelaire's fictions with intent. A parody of this double consciousness is provided by *Actor Posing in Front of a Mirror*, which highlights a comical little anecdote, "The Mirror." Here we consider disguises, moral hypocrisy, and various forms of complacency and self-satisfaction. But the fable's lesson is more complex, as formulated in a legal conundrum. Responding to the ugly man who asserts his right to admire himself in the mirror, the narrator states irreconcilable perspectives: "According to common sense, I was probably right; but, from the legal viewpoint, he was not wrong." That aporia is irony itself, for both positions remain legitimate. Furthermore, even the categories of right and wrong are ambiguous while remaining relevant. The mirror of reality becomes an instrument of deception.

Finally, works by Constantin Guys, whom Baudelaire called "the painter of modern life," return us to the fables' historical origins. Baudelaire's striking but ephemeral fictions of contemporary life, full of surprising encounters and turns of thought, effectively convey the "presentness" of his era. I placed Guys's rather frivolous *Two Gentlemen and a Lady* next to "Portraits of Mistresses," one of the more elaborate stories, which corresponds, in an idiom of maturity, to "Vocations." The Guys image becomes ironic since the fable's graceful woman is murdered by one of the men, simply "because *she was perfect*"—a fierce literalization indeed of temporality and imperfection.

The most delicate pictorial irony, however, is provided by *A Lady of Fashion,* a counterpoint to "Miss Scalpel," Baudelaire's most advanced ethical (and religious) parable. Guys depicts a self-satisfied young woman, while the heroine of "Miss Scalpel" is a mature but mentally ill person with whom the Parisian Prowler strives unsuccessfully to communicate. The model's alluring insouciance provides a foil to the narrator's desperate prayer at the fable's ending: "Lord, have pity, take pity on madmen and madwomen! O Creator! Can monsters exist in the eyes of the only One who knows why they exist, how they *were made* and how they might have been able *not to be made?*" Human understanding can neither fathom the ultimate purpose of good and evil nor justify the suffering of innocent people. God's meaning remains elusive, beyond the mystery.

*The Parisian Prowler* ends, nevertheless, with an affirmation. Baudelaire contends that art can foster community. Irony gives way to sincerity in the final fable, "The Good Dogs," introduced by Bracquemond's etching of a modest painting by Joseph Stevens. (Baudelaire dedicated this lyrical piece, without ironic intent, to Stevens, who aided him during his miserable self-imposed exile in Brussels.) The prose poem is itself a literal (and literary) act of gratitude to "the painter [who] shed his vest on behalf of the poet," rhythmically celebrating "the muddied dog, the poor dog, the homeless dog, the stroller dog, the acrobat dog"—all avatars of the itinerant author himself.

Placing Bracquemond's etching before the fiftieth fable effects a reconciliation between the author and his harried illustrator. Baudelaire had rejected several versions of Bracquemond's frontispiece for the 1861 (second) edition of *Les Fleurs du Mal* before accepting a portrait.

Compassion and friendship (and his special fascination

with "women past their prime"), we might conclude, are the heartbeat of the mature Baudelaire's inspiration. The Bracquemond/Stevens illustration reinforces the poet's cordial self-expression and places a decisive ethical seal on the collection as a whole.

The last vignette—the widely reproduced *Le Stryge* (gargoyle) by Charles Méryon—pays further tribute to a friend. Placed after the notes and the illustration credits, it resorts to the dissident poet of tradition. Baudelaire had asked Méryon to illustrate his anticipated collection of prose poems— or whatever he intended to call them. But the artist's periodic episodes of psychosis became so acute that he fell into a severe breakdown before Baudelaire—a more functional neurotic—could consummate the collaboration.

This graphic closure recognizes Méryon's good intentions, and my translation ends by expressing thanks to Baudelaire's past editors. English-speaking readers can finish the book by contemplating the conventional emblem of *Le Spleen de Paris,* long familiar to the French.

Finally, as my then three-year-old son suggested to me by imitating the gargoyle, this magnificent monster of Notre Dame also reminds us that Baudelaire as well, precariously ensconced at the height of his immortality, sticks out his tongue at the self-satisfied readers and interpreters we all strive to become.

*Edward K. Kaplan*

# INTRODUCTION
## Baudelaire's Neglected Masterpiece

The reputation of Charles Baudelaire (1821–67) remains ambiguous more than a century after his death: Catholic or Satanist, heroic or depraved, idealist or realist? Baudelaire was a brilliant art critic, a theoretician of modernity, and a poet who launched a European literary revolution. He is still remembered as the scandalous author of *Les Fleurs du Mal*, commonly translated as *The Flowers of Evil*, the immediate impact of which derives from its focus on deviant forms of loving and emotional turmoil. Published in 1857, the same year as Flaubert's *Madame Bovary*, Baudelaire's masterwork—the poet's "first revolution"—marks the boundary between romanticism and what we know as the modern era.

Unfortunately, the Establishment did not understand this shift in consciousness. After the brutally repressed upheavals of 1848, the government censored literature more actively than ever. Flaubert's innovative novel was brought to court in January 1857 for its objective depiction of adultery; *Les Fleurs du Mal* was confiscated by judicial order on 7 July, a scant fortnight after its publication, and six poems were condemned on 20 August. Baudelaire was stunned that the public could not appreciate the "horrifying morality" of his portraits of contemporary spiritual and social life; readers resisted his subversion of romantic utopianism.

Despite this violent blow to his ambitions, Baudelaire revised *Les Fleurs du Mal*, and its second edition in 1861 inaugurated his "second revolution." Thirty-two added poems—and the new section, "Parisian Pictures"—radically question transcendent Beauty in favor of everyday reality. This literary conversion nourished Baudelaire's critical writings as well. His famous essay on Constantin Guys, "The Painter of Modern Life," written about 1860, goes far beyond its appreciation of the artist to locate contemporary "beauty" in "its essential quality of presentness."

It was during that period that Baudelaire founded his unique "prose poems" (as he tentatively labeled them), which depict the *flâneur*, or incognito stroller, sketched in his essay on Guys. *The Parisian Prowler*—as I entitle the collection—represents, in the words of Georges Blin, an "absolute beginning." Consisting of fifty "fables of modern life," it is Baudelaire's neglected masterpiece.

The poet first experimented with prose and verse doublets in 1855, but they soon developed as a completely independent genre. In 1857 he published six "nocturnal poems," and in 1861 there appeared a sequence of nine "prose poems," the first to be named as such. The twenty-six pieces printed for the newspaper *La Presse* in 1862 remained definitive. During his waning years, his physical and mental health undermined by his previously dormant syphilis, the poet had organized a table of contents, which his first editors, Charles Asselineau and Théodore de Banville, faithfully followed in their posthumous edition. But few readers recognized *Le Spleen de Paris: Petits Poèmes en prose* as an innovation of equal magnitude to *Les Fleurs du Mal*.

Historically we might locate *The Parisian Prowler* somewhere between Edgar Allan Poe's fantastic tales, which Baudelaire translated, and the enigmatic parables and paradoxes of Franz Kafka, which anticipate postmodern subversions of literature's meaning, and the "theoretical fables" of Jorge Luis Borges, allegories of fiction itself. Baudelaire's fables include several subgenres that dramatize, as the author wrote, "modern life, or rather *one* modern and more abstract life"—the mind and sensibility of their acutely self-conscious narrator.

Baudelaire's "prose poems" are not, despite the generic label, lyrical prose harmonizing rhythm and imagery with a

story line. Before him, Jean-Jacques Rousseau and Chateaubriand had effectively embedded picturesque tableaux
into their voluminous narratives. Aloysius Bertrand's *Gaspard de la nuit,* which Baudelaire slyly claimed had inspired his project, cannot account for his unique polyphony
of styles and attitudes: poetic empathy with ironic detach-
ment, analysis with mystical participation in cosmic harmony, parody, and solemn parable.

These sometimes incompatible pieces are unified by a
figure of Charles Baudelaire himself—a city writer yearning
to reconcile his vision of the Absolute with the imperfect
reality he can never deny. Paris of the 1850s, soon to be
demolished and "renovated" by Napoleon III's prefect,
Baron Haussmann, is his stage. Each character reflects the
narrator-artist's struggles to buttress his integrity. Pitiful acrobats (or *saltimbanques*) excite his compassion, as do old or
middle-aged women who maintain, as he does, dreams of
companionship despite insistent evidence they will never be
fulfilled. The tall, majestic widow (of fable no. 13), pen-
sively holding her little boy's hand, evokes Baudelaire's
childlike nostalgia for his idealized mother, an attractive
thirty-five-year-old woman who remarried all too swiftly after
his father's death. One can imagine that the four boys of
"Vocations" (no. 31) anticipate the four middle-aged bachelors, in "Portraits of Mistresses" (no. 42), proxies of the
graying author who, at his climacteric age, despite chronic
disillusion, bravely seeks "something [he] can love and
respect."

*The Parisian Prowler* possesses an architecture compar-
able to that claimed for *Les Fleurs du Mal.* Some readers
emphasize their contradictions, impressed with disparities
within individual fables, and the obvious variety of the whole.
Yet, in translating these works while writing a book-length
critical analysis, I repeatedly confirmed their consistency,
within small groups and within the overall progression. An
integral reading is justified by the author's handwritten
memorandum which deliberately numbers fifty pieces—a

quantity appropriate to a coherent work—and preserves the order of previously published sequences.

Each fable contributes to the narrator's restless search for community and family. His quest begins with clashes between fantasy and reality and reaches the threshold of meaninglessness and despair. It ends, however, in the final piece, with a literary act of friendship.

Yet this is no *Divine Comedy* in which the exemplary poet, guided by human wisdom and God's grace, acknowledges and purges his frailty. Quite the contrary. Our postromantic guide is an alienated intellectual, a metaphysical exile, an irremediable bachelor, a lonely, jobless, but peripatetic writer who endures the contradictions of his transitional age. No single attitude stabilizes the Parisian Prowler's volatile temperament, and he appears frequently to repudiate norms of charity, social equality, or even the artistic quest for perfection. A careful reading will reveal his attacks against all sorts of pretense and self-delusion to be Socratic challenges to his "hypocritical readers." The narrator's irony masks with a mordant skepticism his compassion for those who live at the margins.

The last four fables (nos. 47–50) summarize, and then surpass, the great themes of imaginative escape, urban anthropology, poetry, and love, which inspirit *The Parisian Prowler*. The narrator of "Miss Scalpel" beseeches a silent God to justify undeserved suffering. "Any Where Out of the World"—Baudelaire's poetic manifesto—confesses to the suicidal restlessness which sometimes invigorates reverie. The outrageous "Let's Beat Up the Poor!" epitomizes the gallows humor of those "immoral" tales which claim that another person's pain is a trivial price to pay for a theoretical truth. The long, lyrical meditation closing the collection—"The Good Dogs"—asserts, with a rare candor, that literature can repay friendship.

Still, these modern fables undermine any reassuring interpretations. Dismantling all forms of complacency and idealism, the Baudelairean "prose poem" amalgamates, in a dialogically open-ended literary unit, ambiguity and judgment, kindness and cruelty, anger and generosity, reverie and analysis. There are no definitive lessons—only responses. In the end, we must judge for ourselves.

## THIS EDITION AND TRANSLATION

As translator, I have attempted to preserve both philological accuracy and literary tact. My approach differs significantly from the two important translations, each published at forty year intervals, preceding mine. Arthur Symons's pioneering rendition of the *Poems in Prose* (London: Mathews, 1905) and Louise Varèse's *Paris Spleen* (New York: New Directions, 1947) tend toward British ornate style and retain many Gallicisms, respecting the notion (which I reject) that the "prose poems" are predominantly "poetic" and "romantic." I have tried to render Baudelaire in present-day English.

These modern fables include a troubled harmony of tones and styles: humorous and colloquial, or pedantic and systematically flat—and only exceptionally rhythmic or lyrical. Avoiding Latinate words and syntax where the French tends toward everyday usage, I nevertheless preserved intricate word order and formality when found in the original. My goal was to maintain a fable's irony—when I perceived it—without reducing its ambiguity. Most of the important puns have been preserved, as has the monotony of repeated key words. Baudelaire often fought with his editors to retain commas, and I have usually seconded his battles. The slow reading which often results, I believe, better maintains *The Parisian Prowler*'s vitality.

I follow the impeccable Pichois edition (Paris: Gallimard, Pléiade, *Oeuvres complètes* I, 1975), which I coordinated with the Kopp critical edition (Paris: Corti, 1969). Readers familiar with these authoritative French versions will notice three departures from tradition.

First, my title, *The Parisian Prowler* ("Le Rôdeur parisien"), found in a letter Baudelaire wrote to Arsène Houssaye (Christmas, 1861), never appeared in print. Robert Kopp retained the title of the 1862 *La Presse* series, *Petits Poèmes en prose*, with "Le Spleen de Paris" as subtitle. Claude Pichois chose *Le Spleen de Paris*, which evokes the grim tone of many pieces, followed by the generic designation, "Petits Poèmes en prose." I find that the title *Paris Spleen* overemphasizes the depressive aspects while "Little prose poems" highlights the ancillary problem of rhythmic style which has diverted many critics. *The Parisian Prowler*, despite shortcomings, typifies more than any other title Baudelaire considered, the intellectually curious, though alienated, narrator's repeated journeys of initiation. It also differentiates this translation from its predecessors.

Placing Baudelaire's "Letter to Arsène Houssaye" in an appendix, rather than at the head, is the second significant change. This precocious "preface" to the 1862 *La Presse* series states the author's intentions—but in an elusive form. Sparring with Houssaye, an obtuse editor, journalist, and mediocre author, Baudelaire had not yet foreseen his prose poems' extraordinary innovations. The first two fables, "The Stranger" and "The Old Woman's Despair," define the collection's fundamental themes and serve as a fit introduction.

Finally, I have included illustrations by artists whom Baudelaire admired and wrote about in his essays on esthetics, as well as two drawings by the author himself. He had asked Charles Meryon to contribute engravings related to Paris for an eventual collection, but the artist fell insane before the collaboration could begin. The pictures I have chosen are intended to parallel the fables and to enhance, not restrict, the openness of interpretation. I hope that English-speaking readers will discover in this version of *The Parisian Prowler* a worthy companion to *Les Fleurs du Mal*, Baudelaire's poetic masterpiece.

*Edward K. Kaplan*

The Parisian Prowler

# THE STRANGER

"Tell me, whom do you love the most, you enigmatic man? your father, your mother, your sister, or your brother?"

"I have neither father, nor mother, nor sister, nor brother."

"Your friends?"

"There you use a word whose meaning until now has remained to me unknown."

"Your fatherland?"

"I am unaware in what latitude it lies."

"Beauty?"

"I would willingly love her, goddess and immortal."

"Gold?"

"I hate it as you hate God."

"So! Then what do you love, you extraordinary stranger?"

"I love clouds... drifting clouds... there... over there... marvelous clouds!"

Imp. Delâtre Rue St Jacques. 171.

# THE OLD WOMAN'S DESPAIR

The shriveled little old woman felt quite delighted when she saw the pretty baby whom everyone was entertaining, and whom everyone was trying to please; a pretty creature, as fragile as she, the little old woman, and, like her as well, toothless and without hair.                                    *(NHUMAN)*

And she went up to him, trying to make little smiles and pleasant faces at him.

But the terrified child struggled under the kind decrepit woman's caresses, and filled the house with his yelpings.

Then the kind old woman withdrew into her eternal solitude, and she wept alone in a corner, saying to herself, "Ah, for us, unfortunate old females that we are, the age of pleasing has passed, even innocent creatures; and we disgust little children we try to love!"

*ARTIFICIALITY = INBORN IN*
*THE CITY INFANT*

# THE ARTIST'S *CONFITEOR*

How penetrating are the ends of autumn days! Ah! penetrating to the verge of pain! For there are certain delicious sensations whose vagueness does not exclude intensity; and there is no sharper point than Infinity.

Sheer delight to drown one's gaze in the immensity of sky and sea! Solitude, silence, incomparable chastity of the azure! a small sail trembling on the horizon, and whose smallness and isolation imitate my irremediable existence, monotonous melody of the swell—all these things think through me, or I think through them (for in the grandeur of reverie, the *self* is quickly lost!). They think, I say, but musically and pictorially, without quibblings, without syllogisms, without deductions.

However, these thoughts, whether they emerge from me or spring from things, soon grow too intense. The force of voluptuous pleasure creates uneasiness and concrete suffering. Then my excessively taut nerves produce nothing but shrill and painful vibrations.

And now the sky's depth fills me with dismay; its limpidity exasperates me. The sea's insensitivity, the scene's immutability appall me... Ah! must we suffer eternally, or else eternally flee the beautiful? Nature, sorceress without mercy, ever victorious rival, let me be! Stop tempting my desires and my pride! Studying the beautiful is a duel in which the artist shrieks with fright before being defeated.

# A JOKER

It was the New Year's Eve explosion: chaos of mud and snow, *PRIMORDEAL*
crisscrossed by a thousand carriages, glittering with toys
and candy, swarming with cupidities and despairs, official
big city dementia fashioned to disturb the brain of the most
steadfast solitary.

Amidst this hubbub and racket, a donkey was trotting
briskly along, pestered by a lout armed with a whip.

Just as the donkey was about to turn a sidewalk corner, a
handsome gloved gentleman, polished, cruelly cravated and
imprisoned in brand-new clothes, bowed obsequiously to
the humble beast, and said to him, as he raised his hat, "I
wish you a good and happy one!" then turned with a fatuous
look toward some companions or other, as if requesting them
to add their approval to his conceit.

The donkey did not see that fine joker, and continued
zealously to rush along where his duty called him.

As for me, suddenly I was seized with an incommensur-
able rage against that magnificent imbecile, who for me con-
centrated in himself the very essence of France's wit.

*R -EVOLUTION*

# THE DOUBLE ROOM

A room that resembles a reverie, a truly *spiritual* room, where the stagnant atmosphere is lightly tinged with pink and blue.

Here the soul takes a bath of laziness, perfumed with regret and desire. —Something like twilight, bluish and pinkish; a dream of voluptuous pleasure during an eclipse.

The furniture has elongated, collapsed, languid shapes. The furniture seems to be dreaming, you might say endowed with a somnambular life, like vegetables and minerals. The fabrics speak a silent language, like flowers, like skies, like setting suns.

No artistic abomination on the walls. Compared to pure dream, to unanalyzed impressions, a precise art, a concrete art, is blasphemy. Everything here possesses the abundant light and delicious darkness of harmony.

An infinitesimal scent of the most exquisite choice, mingled with the slightest wetness, swims in that atmosphere, where the drowsy mind is lulled by hothouse sensations.

Muslin rains abundantly over the windows and before the bed; it pours in snowy waterfalls. On this bed lies the Idol, the sovereign queen of dreams. But how did she get here? Who brought her? What magic power set her on this throne of reverie and voluptuousness? What difference does it make? Here she is and I recognize her!

These are indeed the eyes whose flame pierces the twilight; those subtle and terrifying *peepers*, which I recognize by their frightful malice! They attract, they subjugate, they devour the gaze of anyone reckless enough to contemplate them. I have often studied them, those black stars summoning curiosity and admiration.

What benevolent demon has thus surrounded me with mystery, silence, peace, and aromas? O beatitude! What we usually call life, even in its most favorable expansion, has nothing in common with this supreme life of which I am now conscious and which I relish minute by minute, second by second!

*BEAUTY = NON-TEMPORAL*

No! There are no more minutes, there are no more seconds! Time has disappeared. Eternity now reigns, an eternity of delights!

But then an awful, heavy knock resounded on the door, and, just like in a bedeviled dream, I felt a pickax strike me in the stomach.

And then a Specter entered. He is a bailiff come to torture me in the name of the law; a loathsome concubine come to bemoan her poverty and adding the trivialities of her life to the sorrows of mine; or even a newspaper editor's errand boy calling for the manuscript's next installment.

The paradisiacal room, the idol, the sovereign queen of dreams, the *Sylphid*, as the big René used to say, all that magic disappeared at the Specter's brutal blow.

Dreadful! I remember! Yes I remember! This hovel, this abode of eternal ennui, is truly mine. See the furniture, stupid, dusty, chipped; the hearth without fire or embers, soiled with spit; the dreary windows where rain has traced furrows in the dust; the manuscripts, scratched up or unfinished; the calendar where the menacing dates are marked in pencil!

And that scent of another world, which I used to intoxicate myself with a perfected sensitivity, alas! it was replaced by a fetid odor of tobacco mixed with some sort of nauseating mustiness. Now you breathe a rancid smell of destitution.

Here in this world, narrow but so filled with disgust, only one familiar object cheers me: the vial of laudanum, an old

*UNCANNY*

and terrifying friend, and like all woman friends, alas! fertile in caresses and betrayals!

Yes indeed! Time has reappeared; Time reigns as sovereign now. And with that hideous old man the whole diabolical procession has returned, Memories, Regrets, Spasms, Fears, Anguishes, Nightmares, Rages, and Neuroses.

Now I find the seconds strongly and solemnly intensified, and, bursting from the clock, each one says, "I am Life, unbearable, relentless Life!"

There is but one Second in human life whose mission it is to announce good news, the *good news* that causes everyone such inexplicable fear.

Yes! Time reigns; it has recaptured its brutal dictatorship. And it drives me, as if I were an ox, with its double goad. —"So gee'up! donkey! So sweat, slave! So live, damned one!"

*DREAMS — NON-TEMPORAL,*
*— PURE BEAUTY*
*— TRANSCENDANT*

# TO EACH HIS CHIMERA

Under a huge gray sky, on a huge dusty plain, without paths, without grass, without a thistle, without a nettle, I came upon several men walking along bent over.

Each of them was carrying an enormous Chimera on his back, as heavy as a sack of flour or coal, or the rig of a Roman footsoldier.

Yet the monstrous beast was not an inert weight. On the contrary, she enwrapped and subjugated the man with flexible and powerful muscles; with her two huge claws she hooked onto the breast of her mount; and her fabled head topped the man's forehead, like one of those ghastly helmets which ancient warriors hoped would increase their enemy's terror.

I questioned one of these men, and I asked him where they were going like that. He answered that he knew nothing about it, not he, nor the others; but that obviously they were going somewhere, since they were driven by an irresistible need to walk.

A curious thing to note: none of these travelers seemed bothered by the ferocious beast hanging around his neck and attached to his back. They seemed to consider it as part of themselves. All their weary and serious faces expressed no sign of despair. Under the sky's splenetic dome, their feet immersed in the dust of a terrain as ravaged as the sky, they made their way with the resigned expression of those who are condemned to hope forever.

And the procession passed by me and descended into the

horizon's atmosphere, at that place where the planet's rounded surface hides from the curiosity of the human gaze.

And for a few moments I persistently tried to understand this mystery. But soon insurmountable Apathy swooped down upon me, and I was more heavily oppressed than they were themselves by their overwhelming Chimeras.

# THE FOOL AND THE VENUS

What an admirable day! The vast park swoons under the sun's blazing eye, like youth under Love's domination.

The universal ecstasy of things declares itself without noise; the very waters seem to sleep. Quite unlike human celebrations, here is a silent orgy.

An ever-increasing light seems to make objects increasingly sparkle. Aroused flowers burn with the desire to outdo the sky's azure by the energy of their colors, and the heat, turning scents visible, seems to make them rise to the stars like smoke.

However, amidst this universal rapture, I noticed an afflicted creature.

At the feet of a colossal Venus, one of those artificial fools, one of those voluntary buffoons assigned to make kings laugh when pursued by Remorse or Ennui, rigged out in a flashy and ridiculous costume, capped in horns and bells, all heaped against the pedestal, raises his tear-filled eyes toward the immortal Goddess.

And his eyes say, "I am the lowest and the most lonely of humans, deprived of love and of friendship, and for that reason quite inferior to the most incomplete animals. However I am made, I as well, to understand and to feel immortal Beauty! Oh Goddess! take pity on my sorrow and my madness!"

But the implacable Venus looks into the distance at something or other with her eyes of marble.

# THE DOG
# AND THE SCENT-BOTTLE

"My beautiful dog, my nice dog, my dear bowwow, come here and inhale an excellent perfume purchased from the best perfumer in the city."

And the dog, wagging its tail, which is, I believe, among those poor creatures, the sign corresponding to laughter and smiles, comes near and, curious, puts its wet nose on the unstoppered bottle. Then suddenly recoiling in terror, it barks at me, by way of reproach.

"Ah miserable dog! If I had offered you a lump of excrement, you would have sniffed it with delight and perhaps devoured it. Because of this, you, unworthy companion of my dreary life, you resemble the public, which must never be offered delicate perfumes that exasperate them, but only meticulously selected garbage."

# THE BAD GLAZIER

There exist characters, purely contemplative and completely unsuited for action, who, however, influenced by a mysterious and unknown impulse, sometimes act with a speed of which they would not have believed themselves capable.

Such as the one who, dreading to find distressing news with his concierge, prowls cravenly around her door for an hour without daring to enter; the one who saves a letter for two weeks without opening it, or only after six months gives in and completes a task necessary a year before. These people sometimes feel abruptly hurled into action by an irresistible force, like an arrow out of a bow. The moralist and the physician, who claim to know everything, cannot explain the cause of this crazy energy which hits these lazy and voluptuous souls so suddenly, and how, incapable of carrying out the simplest and the most necessary things, one minute later they find an excess courage for executing the most absurd and often even the most dangerous acts.

One of my friends, the most harmless dreamer who ever existed, once set a forest on fire to see—so he said—if fire would catch as easily as people generally assert. Ten times in a row, the experiment failed; but the eleventh time, it succeeded all too well.

Another would light a cigar next to a powder keg, *to see, to know, to tempt fate,* forcing himself to display proof of energy, to play the gambler, to experience the pleasures of anxiety, for nothing, through caprice, from idleness.

It is the type of energy that springs from ennui and daydreaming; and those in whom it arises so unexpectedly are, generally, as I said, the most indolent and dreamiest of creatures.

Another one, so shy that he drops his eyes even before a man's gaze, and must summon up his entire pitiful will to enter a café or pass before a theater box office, where he imagines the ticket takers to be invested with the majesty of Minos, of Aeacus, and Rhadamanthus. He would abruptly hug around the neck an old man walking beside him and kiss him enthusiastically before the astonished crowd.

Why? Because... because he found his expression irresistibly likeable? Perhaps; but it is more legitimate to assume that he himself does not know why.

More than once I have been victim of such attacks and outbursts, which justify our belief that some malicious Demons slip into us and, without us knowing it, make us carry out their most absurd wishes.

One morning I had awakened sullen, sad, and worn out with idleness, and I felt impelled to do something great, a brilliant action. And I opened the window, alas!

(Notice, if you please, that the spirit of mystification which, among certain persons, does not result from effort or scheming, but from a chance inspiration, if only because of the desire's fervor, has much in common with that humor, hysterical according to physicians, satanic according to those who think a little more lucidly than physicians, which drives us irresistibly toward a multitude of dangerous or improper actions.)

The first person I noticed on the street was a glazier, whose piercing, discordant cry reached me through the heavy and dirty Parisian atmosphere. Moreover, it would be impossible for me to say why I was seized by a hatred for this pitiful man as sudden as it was despotic.

"Hey! Hey!" I shouted for him to come up. Meanwhile I was thinking, not without some gaiety, that, since my room was on the seventh floor and the staircase quite narrow, the man must be experiencing some difficulty in effecting his ascent and bumping the corners of his fragile merchandise many times.

He finally appeared. Curiously I examined all his glass, and I told him, "What? You have no colored panes? no pink panes, no red, no blue, no magic panes, no panes of paradise? You are shameless! You dare walk through poor neighborhoods, and you don't even have panes which make life beautiful!" And vigorously I pushed him to the stairs, where he staggered grumbling.

I went to the balcony and I grabbed a little pot of flowers, and when the man reappeared at the door entrance, I let my engine of war drop down perpendicularly on the back edge of his pack. The shock knocked him over, and he ended by breaking his entire poor itinerant fortune under his back, which produced the brilliant sound of a crystal palace smashed by lightning.

And, drunk with my madness, I shouted at him furiously, "Make life beautiful! Make life beautiful!"

Such neurotic pranks are not without peril, and one can often pay dearly for them. But what does an eternity of damnation matter to someone who has experienced for one second the infinity of delight?

# AT ONE O'CLOCK
# IN THE MORNING

Finally alone! Now only the rattling of some lingering and exhausted carriages can still be heard. For a few hours, we will possess silence, if not rest. Finally! The tyranny of the human face has disappeared, and now only I myself will make me suffer.

Finally! So I'm allowed to relax in a bath of darkness! First, a double turn in the lock. I think this turn of the key will increase my solitude and fortify the barricades at present separating me from the world.

Dreadful life! Dreadful city! Let's summarize the day: saw several men of letters, one of whom asked me if you could get to Russia by land (he probably thought Russia was an island); argued generously with a journal editor, who answered to each objection, "Here we are on the side of respectability," implying that all the other papers are run by scoundrels; greeted about twenty persons, fifteen of whom I didn't know; distributed handshakes in the same proportion, and without even the precaution of buying gloves; to kill time, during a downpour, went to see a girl acrobat who asked me to sketch her a *Venustre* costume; paid my respects to a theater director, who said as he was getting rid of me, "It would probably be useful to speak to Z——, he's the dullest, the stupidest and the most famous of all my authors, perhaps with him you might get somewhere. See him, and then we'll see." Boasted (why?) of several bad deeds I never committed, and cravenly denied some other wrongs I carried out with joy, an offense of vainglory, a crime against conventionality. Refused an easy favor to a friend, and gave a written recommendation to a perfect idiot. Phew! Is that all?

Annoyed with everyone and annoyed with myself, I long to redeem myself and to bolster my pride a bit in the silence and solitude of the night. Souls of those I have loved, souls of those I have sung, fortify me, sustain me, remove me from untruth and the world's corrupting fumes. And you, Lord my God! Grant me the grace to produce a few beautiful verses to prove to myself that I am not the lowest of men, and that I am not inferior to those I despise!

# THE WILD WOMAN
# AND THE AFFECTED COQUETTE

"Really, my darling, you weary me beyond measure and without pity. Hearing you sighing, people would think you suffer more than sexagenarian bag ladies and the old beggar women who pick up crusts of bread at tavern doors.

"At least if your sighs expressed remorse, they would do you some honor; but they convey only the satiation of well-being and the exhaustion of leisure. And besides, you never stop pouring yourself out in useless words: 'Love me well! I need it so much! Console me here, caress me there!' All right, I'll try to cure you. We may find the way, for two pennies, at a fair, and without traveling too far.

"Carefully consider, if you please, that massive iron cage where a hairy monster frets about, howls like one of the damned, shakes the bars like an orangutan infuriated by exile, copying to perfection, sometimes the tiger's circular leaps, sometimes the stupid waddling of polar bears, and whose form rather vaguely resembles yours.

"That monster is one of those animals generally called 'my angel!' that is to say, a woman. The other monster, the one screaming his head off, brandishing a club, is a husband. He has chained his legitimate wife like a beast, and displays her in the city outskirts, at fairs, with permission of the authorities, of course.

"Look closely! Observe how voraciously (perhaps not feigned!) she rips apart the living rabbits and squealing fowls her mahout throws to her. He tells her, 'Let's go, you can't eat your fill in one day,' and, with that wise proverb, he cruelly snatches her prey, whose unwound guts remain stuck an instant in the ferocious beast's teeth, I mean the woman's.

"Go to it! A good blow of the club to calm her! for she shoots her ferociously covetous eyes on the snatched-away food. Great God! That club is not a comedian's club, and did you hear her flesh reverberate, despite the fake hair? So her eyes now bulge from her head, and she howls *more naturally*. In her rage, she throws off sparks everywhere, like beaten iron.

"Such are the conjugal customs of these two descendants of Eve and Adam, these works of your hands, O my God! That woman is indisputably unhappy, though after all, perhaps, fame's titillating delights are not unknown to her. There are more irremediable misfortunes, and without compensation. But in the world into which she has been flung, she could never believe that women deserve another destiny.

"Now, let's duel it out, dear precious one! Given the hells populating the world, what do you want me to think of your pretty hell, you who repose only upon fabrics as soft as your skin, who eat only cooked meat, and for whom a clever servant takes care to slice the morsels?

"And what could all those little sighs swelling your perfumed bosom mean to me, robust coquette? And all those affectations learned from books, and that tireless melancholy, fit to arouse in a spectator any feeling other than pity? In fact, I sometimes yearn to teach you what real unhappiness is.

"To see you like this, my delicate beauty, feet in the mire and eyes turned swooningly toward the sky, as if asking a king of it, you convincingly seem like a young frog invoking the ideal. If you scorn this log (which I am now, as you well know), watch out for the crane *which will crunch you, swallow you, and kill you at its pleasure!*

"However much of a poet I am, I'm not as gullible as you

— 19 —

would like to believe, and if you irk me too often with your *precious* whinings, I'll treat you like a *wild woman*, or I'll throw you out the window, like an empty bottle."

# CROWDS

Not everyone is capable of taking a bath of multitude: enjoy-
ing crowds is an art. And only he who can go on a binge of
vitality, at the expense of the human species, is he into
whom in his cradle a fairy breathed a craving for disguises
and masks, hatred of home, and a passion for traveling.

Multitude, solitude: equal and interchangeable terms for
the active and fertile poet. He who does not know how to
populate his solitude, does not know either how to be alone
in a busy crowd.

The poet enjoys the incomparable privilege of being able,
at will, to be himself and an other. Like those wandering
souls seeking a body, he enters, when he wants, into everyone's character. For him alone, everything is empty. And if
certain places seem to exclude him, it is because he considers them not worth the bother of being visited.

The solitary and thoughtful stroller draws a unique intoxication from this universal communion. He who easily es-
pouses crowds knows feverish delights, of which the selfish
will be eternally deprived, locked up like a chest, and the
lazy, confined like a mollusk. He adopts as his every profession, every joy and every misery circumstances place before
him.

What people call love is awfully small, awfully restricted,
and awfully weak, compared with that ineffable orgy, that
holy prostitution of the soul which gives itself totally, poetry
and charity, to the unexpected which appears, to the unknown which passes by.

It is sometimes right to teach the world's happy ones, if

only to humiliate their stupid pride for an instant, that there are forms of happiness superior to theirs, more vast and more refined. Founders of colonies, shepherds of peoples, missionary priests exiled to the ends of the earth, probably know something of these mysterious intoxications. And, in the bosom of the vast family created by their genius, they must sometimes laugh at those who pity their fortunes so troubled and their lives so chaste.

# 13

# WIDOWS

Vauvenargues says that public gardens have pathways haunted mainly by disappointed ambition, unfortunate inventors, thwarted fame, shattered hearts, by all those tumultuous and secretive souls in whom a storm's final sighs still rumble, and who retreat far from the insolent gaze of the joyous and the idle. These shady refuges are meeting places for those maimed by life.

Poets and philosophers love to direct their avid speculations especially toward those places. A guaranteed fodder is there. For if there is anywhere they despise to visit, as I was just implying, it is above all the joy of rich people. That unruliness in a vacuum has nothing to attract them. On the contrary, they feel irresistibly swept toward everything that is weak, ruined, saddened, orphaned.

A practiced eye is never wrong. In those rigid or dejected features, in those hollow and dull eyes, or eyes shining with the battle's final flares, in those deep and numerous wrinkles, in those so slow or so spasmodic gaits, it immediately deciphers innumerable legends of love deceived, of unrecognized devotion, of unrewarded efforts, of hunger and cold humbly, silently, endured.

Have you sometimes noticed widows on those lonely benches, impoverished widows? Whether or not they are wearing mourning, they are easy to recognize. Besides, something is always missing in the poor's mourning clothes, an absence of harmony that makes them more heartbreaking. The poor are forced to skimp on their sorrow. The rich wear theirs in full force.

Which widow is the sadder and the more saddening, the one who drags by the hand a little kid with whom she cannot share her reverie, or the one who is completely alone? I don't know... I once happened to spend long hours following an old afflicted woman of that kind. Stiff, erect, wearing a worn-out little shawl, she maintained in her entire being a stoic pride.

She was obviously condemned, by her absolute solitude, to an old bachelor's habits, and the masculine character of her behavior added a mysterious piquancy to its austerity. I do not know in which wretched café and how she lunched. I followed her into a reading room; and I watched her closely for a long time as she hunted through local papers, with active eyes, once scalded by tears, for some news of intense and personal interest.

Finally, in the afternoon, under a charming autumn sky, one of those skies from which crowds of regrets and memories descend, she sat off in a park, far from the crowd, to hear one of those concerts whose regimental music gladdens the Parisian populace.

This was probably the little debauchery of that innocent old woman (or that purified old woman), a well-earned consolation of one of those oppressive days without friends, without chatting, without joy, without a confidant, which God allowed to fall on her three hundred sixty-five times a year, perhaps already for many years!

Still another one:

I can never resist throwing a glance, if not universally sympathetic, at least curious, on the crowd of pariahs squeezed up against the fence at a public concert. The band flings festive songs, of triumph or of voluptuous pleasure, through the night. Shimmering dresses trail; glances meet; idle folk, wearied with having done nothing, loll about, pretending lazily to savor the music. Nothing here but riches, happiness; nothing that does not exude and inspire heedlessness and the pleasure of letting life happen; nothing, except the sight of that rabble over there leaning on the outer enclosure, catching a shred of music gratis, carried by the wind, and watching the sparkling forge inside.

That reflection of the joy of the rich in the depths of the eyes of the poor is always an interesting thing. But on that particular day, across that populace dressed in overalls and calico dresses, I noticed a creature whose nobility stood in brilliant contrast to all the surrounding coarseness.

She was a tall, majestic woman, and so noble in her entire bearing, that I cannot recall having seen her peer in collections of aristocratic beauties of the past. A perfume of haughty virtue emanated from her entire person. Her face, sad and thinned, was in perfect accord with the formal mourning in which she was dressed. She, too, like the plebeians with whom she had mixed without seeing them, watched the luminous society with knowing eyes, and she listened while gently nodding her head.

Remarkable vision! I said to myself: "Certainly that kind of poverty, if it is poverty, must not concede to sordid thrift; such a noble face vouches for it. Then why does she remain voluntarily in surroundings where she creates such a brilliant contrast?"

But drawing nearer to her out of curiosity, I thought I guessed the reason. The tall widow was holding the hand of a child dressed in black like herself. However modest the admission, that price was perhaps enough to purchase one of the little creature's needs, better still, a superfluity, a toy.

And she probably walked home, meditating and dreaming, alone, forever alone. For a child is unruly, selfish, without gentleness and without patience; and he cannot even, like a mere animal, like a dog or a cat, serve as a confidant to lonely sorrows.

# THE OLD ACROBAT

Everywhere the vacationing populace was showing off, over-
flowing, rejoicing. It was one of those solemn occasions
which acrobats, stunt makers, animal trainers, and itinerant
shopkeepers rely upon, for a long period, to offset the year's
bad seasons.

On those days the populace seems to forget everything,
sorrow and work; they become like children. The little ones
consider it a day off, the dread of school postponed for
twenty-four hours. The grown-ups consider it an armistice
contracted with life's malevolent forces, a respite from universal disputes and struggles.

Even a man of the world and a man engaged in spiritual
works have difficulty escaping the influence of this plebeian
jubilee. They absorb, against their will, their share of that
heedless atmosphere. As for me, as a true Parisian, I never
fail to inspect all the booths flaunting themselves during
these solemn times.

They were, in fact, engaged in a tremendous competition:
they were screeching, bellowing, howling. It was a blend of
shouts, booms of brass, and explosions of rockets. Gro-
tesques and clowns contorted the features of their sunburnt
faces, toughened by wind, rain, and sun; with the audacity
of actors sure of their results, they hurled witticisms and
jests, whose comic quality was as solid and obvious as Molière's. Muscle men, proud of the hugeness of their limbs,
without foreheads or skulls, like orangutans, majestically
lounged about in tights washed the previous night for the

occasion. Dancing girls, lovely as fairies or princesses, jumped and frolicked under lantern flames which filled their skirts with sparks.

All was light, dust, shouts, joy, commotion. Some spent money, others earned it, both equally joyous. Children hung onto their mothers' skirts to get some candy-stick, or climbed onto their fathers' shoulders to get a better view of a magician dazzling like a god. And circulating everywhere, dominating all the scents, a frying odor which was like that festival's incense.

At the end, at the extreme end of the row of booths, as if, ashamed, he had exiled himself from all those splendors, I saw a pitiful acrobat, stooped, obsolete, decrepit, a human ruin, backed against one of the posts of his shack; a shack more wretched than that of the most mindless savage, and whose adversity was still illumined all too well by two burned-down candles, dripping and smoking.

Everywhere joy, profit, debauchery; everywhere the certainty of tomorrow's bread; everywhere the frenzied explosion of vitality. Here absolute wretchedness, wretchedness rigged out, most horrible, rigged out in comic rags, where necessity, much more than art, had introduced the contrast. He was not laughing, the wretched man! He was not crying, he was not dancing, he was not gesturing, he was not shouting; he was singing no song, neither jolly nor woeful, he was not beseeching. He was mute and motionless. He had given up, he had abdicated. His destiny was done.

But what a deep, unforgettable look he cast over the crowd and the lights, whose moving waves stopped a few steps from his repulsive wretchedness! I felt my throat strangled by the dreadful hand of hysteria, and my sight seemed to be blocked by rebellious tears refusing to fall.

What to do? Why ask the unfortunate man what curiosity, what marvel he had to display in that stinking darkness, behind his torn curtain? In fact, I did not dare; and, although the cause of my timidity might make you laugh, I admit that I was afraid of humiliating him. Finally, just as I had resolved to place in passing some money on part of his platform, hoping that he would guess my intention, a huge backflow of populace, caused by some unknown turmoil, swept me far away.

And, turning around, obsessed by that vision, I tried to analyze my sudden sorrow, and I told myself: I have just seen the image of the old writer who has survived the generation whose brilliant entertainer he was; of the old poet without friends, without family, without children, debased by his wretchedness and the public's ingratitude, and whose booth the forgetful world no longer wants to enter!

# THE CAKE

I was traveling. I was set in a landscape of irresistible grandeur and nobility. Just then something of it probably entered
my soul. My thoughts were fluttering as lightly as the atmosphere. Vulgar passions, such as hatred and worldly love,
now felt as distant as the clouds parading deeply in the
abysses beneath my feet; my soul seemed as vast and pure
as the sky's dome which enveloped me. The recollection of
earthly things reached my heart only weakened and diminished, like the sound of bells of imperceptible animals
grazing afar, quite afar, on another mountain slope. Over
the little motionless lake, black in its immense depth, a
cloud's shadow would sometimes pass, flying across the sky,
like the reflection of an airborne giant's cloak. And I remember that this rare and solemn sensation, caused by a
grand and perfectly silent movement, filled me with a joy
mingled with fear. In short, I felt myself to be in perfect
peace with myself and with the universe, thanks to the im-
passioning beauty encircling me. I even believe that, in my
perfect beatitude and in total forgetfulness of all earthly
evil, I had arrived at the idea of no longer finding so ridiculous the newspapers which claim that people are born
good—until incorrigible matter renewed its demands. Then
I began to think about relieving the fatigue and alleviating
the hunger caused by such a long ascent. I took from my
pocket a big piece of bread, a leather cup and a flask of a
certain elixir that pharmacists sell these days to tourists to
be mixed when needed with melted snow.

As I was placidly cutting my bread, a very slight noise

made me look up. A little ragged creature stood before me, black, disheveled, whose hollow eyes, wild and as if beseeching, were devouring the piece of bread. And I heard him, in a low, hoarse voice, moan the word "*cake!*" I couldn't help laughing when I heard the designation with which he agreed to honor my almost white bread, and so I cut off a fine slice and gave it to him. Slowly he came near, not taking his eyes from the object of his greed. Then, snatching the piece with his hand, he retreated briskly, as if afraid that my offer was not sincere or that I had already regretted making it.

But at the same instant he was knocked over by another little savage, sprung from nowhere, and so perfectly resembling the first that you could take him for his twin brother. They rolled together on the ground, fighting over the precious prey, neither apparently willing to sacrifice his half to his brother. The first one, infuriated, clutched the second by the hair; the other one bit his ear and, with a magnificent swear in dialect, spat out a little bloody piece of it. The cake's legitimate proprietor tried to sink his little claws into the usurper's eyes; the other in turn applied all his strength to strangling his adversary with one hand, while with the other he tried to slip the battle prize into his pocket. But, rekindled by despair, the loser stood straight up and sent the victor sprawling to the ground butting him in the stomach. Why describe a hideous struggle which in fact lasted longer than their childish strength might lead one to expect? Every moment the cake traveled from hand to hand and changed pockets. But alas! it also changed volume. And when they finally stopped from the sheer impossibility of continuing, exhausted, gasping, bleeding, there was no longer, truth to tell, any cause of battle. The piece of bread had disappeared, and its crumbs were scattered like the grains of sand with which it was mixed.

That performance obscured the landscape for me, and the calm joy gladdening my soul before I saw those little men had completely disappeared. I remained saddened for quite a while, and I incessantly repeated to myself: "So there exists a magnificent land where bread is called *cake*, a delicacy so rare that it suffices to beget a perfectly fratricidal war!"

# THE CLOCK

The Chinese tell time in a cat's eyes.

One day, walking in the outskirts of Nanking, a missionary realized he had forgotten his watch, and he asked a little boy what time it was.

At first the kid from the Celestial Empire hesitated; then, reconsidering, he answered, "I am going to tell you." Not many moments later, he reappeared, holding a very fat cat in his arms, and looking at it, as they say, straight in the eye, he asserted without hesitation, "It is not yet quite noon." Which was true.

As for me, if I turn toward beautiful Felina, so well named, who is at once the honor of her sex, my heart's pride and my mind's perfume, whether it be night, whether it be day, in full light or dark shadow, I always see the time clearly, in the depths of her adorable eyes, a vast, solemn time, always the same, huge as space, without divisions into minutes or seconds—an immobile time not marked on clocks, and yet light as a sigh, swift as a glance.

And if some meddler happened to interrupt me while settling my gaze upon that delectable dial, if some rude and intolerant Genie, some Demon of untimeliness happened to ask me, "What are you watching with such care? What are you looking for in that creature's eyes? Do you see the time there, prodigal and lazy mortal?" I would directly answer, "Yes, I see the time; it is Eternity!"

Now is this not, Madam, a truly praiseworthy madrigal, and as exaggerated as yourself? In fact, I took such delight in elaborating this pretentious romance, that I will ask nothing of you in exchange.

# A HEMISPHERE IN TRESSES

Let me inhale ever so long, ever so long, the odor of your hair, plunge my whole face into it, like a thirsting man into the water of a spring, and wave it with my hand like a fragrant handkerchief, stirring memories into the air.

If only you could know everything I see! everything I feel! everything I hear in your hair! My soul travels on aromas like other men's souls on music.

Your hair holds an entire dream, filled with sails and rigging; it holds huge seas whose monsoons carry me toward enchanting climates, where space is bluer and deeper, where the atmosphere is perfumed with fruits, foliage, and human skin.

In the ocean of your tresses, I discern a harbor teeming with melancholy songs, with vigorous men from all nations and ships of all forms outlining their delicate and complicated architecture against an immense sky where basks the eternal heat.

In the strokings of your tresses, I recover the languor of passing long hours on a divan, in the stateroom of a beautiful ship, lulled by the harbor's imperceptible rollings, between flower pots and cooling water jars.

In the fiery hearth of your tresses, I inhale the smell of tobacco mixed with opium and sugar. In the night of your tresses, I see the infinity of the tropical azure glowing. On the downy shores of your tresses I become intoxicated with the mingled smells of tar, musk, and coconut oil.

Let me bite ever so long into your tresses heavy and black. When I nibble at your elastic and unruly hair, I seem to be eating memories.

# 18

# INVITATION TO THE VOYAGE

There exists a magnificent land, a land of Cockaigne, as they say, which I dream of visiting with a familiar confidante. Remarkable land, drowned in the mists of our North, and which we might call the Orient of the West, the China of Europe, so freely does a hearty and capricious fancy flourish there, adorning it so patiently and stubbornly with her learned and delicate vegetation.

A true land of Cockaigne, where everything is beautiful, rich, calm, decent; where excess takes pleasure in mirroring itself in uniformity; where life breathes luxuriant and mellow; where disorder, commotion, and the unexpected are excluded; where happiness is wedded to silence; where even cooking is poetic, both luxuriant and arousing; where everything resembles you, my dear angel.

Do you feel that feverish ailment seizing us in our stark affliction, that longing for unheard-of realms, that anguish of curiosity? A land exists resembling you, where everything is beautiful, rich, calm, and decent; where fancy has built and furnished a western China, where life breathes mellow, where happiness is wedded to silence. There is where we must live, where we must go to die!

Yes, we must go there to breathe, to dream, and to prolong the hours with an infinity of sensations. A musician has written "Invitation to the Waltz." Who then will compose "Invitation to the Voyage," to be presented to the beloved woman, to the favored sister?

Yes, it would be fine to live in that atmosphere—far away, where the slower hours contain more thoughts, where clocks strike happiness with a deeper and more meaningful solemnity.

On glossy panels, or on gilded and darkly rich leathers, blissful pictures live discreetly, quiet and profound, like the souls of the artists who created them. The setting suns, so richly tinting the dining room or the salon, sift through beautiful fabrics or through tall crafted windows divided into many leaded panes. The furniture is huge, unusual, weird, armed with locks and hiding places like refined souls. The mirrors, the metals, the fabrics, the silver, and the porcelain play a silent and secretive symphony for the eyes. And a remarkable aroma escapes from everything, from every corner, from the splits in drawers and the creases of fabrics, a fragrant *spirit* from Sumatra, which seems to be the apartment's soul.

A true land of Cockaigne, I insist, where everything is rich, tidy, and glossy, like a clean conscience, like a magnificent array of kitchen utensils, like splendid silverware, like colorful jewelry! The world's treasures pour in there, as into the house of a hard-working man who deserves the whole world's best. Remarkable land, superior to others, as Art is to Nature, where dream refashions Nature, where it is corrected, embellished, recast.

May they search, continue to search, may they ceaselessly extend the limits of their happiness, those alchemists of horticulture! May they offer prizes of sixty and of one hundred thousand florins for someone to solve their ambitious problems! As for me, I have found my *black tulip* and my *blue dahlia!*

Incomparable flower, rediscovered tulip, allegorical dahlia, isn't it there, to that beautiful land, so quiet and so dreamy, that we must go to live and flourish? Would you not be framed by your analogy there, and could you not mirror yourself, as the mystics say, in your own *correspondence?*

Dreams! always dreams! And the more ambitious and delicate the soul, the more dreams remove it from the possible.

Each of us carries within a dose of natural opium, ceaselessly secreted and renewed; and, from birth to death, how many hours can we count filled with concrete delight, with well-executed and resolute action? Will we ever live, will we ever enter that picture painted by my mind, that painting which resembles you?

These treasures, this furniture, this excess, this uniformity, these scents, these miraculous flowers, they are you. Still you again, these wide rivers and calm canals. The enormous ships they sweep along, loaded full with riches, and from which the crew's monotonous songs ascend, these are my thoughts sleeping or flowing on your breast. You lead them gently toward the sea which is the Infinite, all the while reflecting the sky's depths in the transparency of your lovely soul. —And when they reach the native port, wearied by the waves and glutted on the produce of the East, they are still my enriched thoughts returning from the Infinite toward you.

# 19

# THE PAUPER'S TOY

I want to present an idea about innocent entertainment. For so few diversions are not wicked!

When some morning you go out firmly intending to stroll on the open roads, fill your pockets with small penny devices—such as flat, single-string Punch marionettes, blacksmiths striking their anvil, the rider and his horse whose tail is a whistle—and offer them in tribute to the unknown and poor children you meet, alongside taverns or under trees. You will see their eyes open exorbitantly. First they won't dare take it, doubting their good fortune. Then their hands will briskly grasp the gift, and they'll flee like cats running far away to eat the morsel you have given them, having learned to distrust people.

On a road, behind the grate of a vast garden, where the whiteness of a pretty castle struck by the sun appeared in the background, stood a lovely and spiffy child, dressed in those country clothes so full of affectation.

Luxury, heedlessness, and the habitual spectacle of wealth make those children so pretty that they seem to be made of different stuff from ordinary or poor children.

At his side, on the grass, lay a splendid toy as spiffy as its master, varnished, gilded, wearing a purple dress, and covered with plumes and glass beads. But the child paid no attention to his favorite toy, and this is what he was watching:

On the other side of the grate, on the road, amidst thistles and nettles, stood another child, dirty, puny, grimy, one of those pariah-brats whose beauty an impartial eye might discover, if it could wipe away his repulsive patina of privation, just as a connoisseur's eye detects an ideal painting beneath the coachmaker's varnish.

Across those symbolic bars separating two worlds, the open road and the castle, the poor child was showing his own toy to the rich child who was greedily inspecting it like a rare and unknown object. Now, that toy, which the little scum was poking, turning, and shaking in its grated box, was a living rat! His parents, probably to save money, had extracted the toy from life itself.

And the two children laughed at each other fraternally, with teeth of *equal* whiteness.

# THE FAIRIES' GIFTS

It was the Fairies' high convocation, for conducting the distribution of gifts to all the newborns come into life within the past twenty-four hours.

All these ancient and capricious Sisters of Fate, all these weird Mothers of joy and of sorrow, were quite diverse: some looked sullen and sour, others looked frisky and mischievous; some, young ones who had always been young; others, old ones who had always been old.

All the fathers who believe in Fairies had arrived, each one carrying his newborn in his arms.

Gifts, Faculties, good Chances, insurmountable Circumstances, were piled up beside the rostrum, like prizes on a table at graduation. But what was unusual here was that the Gifts were not the reward of effort, but quite the contrary, a grace granted to someone who had not yet lived, a grace able to decide its fate and become just as easily the source of its misfortune as of its happiness.

The poor Fairies were quite busy, since the crowd of petitioners was large, and this intermediary world, located between mankind and God, is subject like ours to the terrifying law of Time and its infinite descendants, Days, Hours, Minutes, Seconds.

In fact, they were as bewildered as cabinet ministers on hearing days, or pawnshop employees when a national holiday allows gratis redemptions. I even think they glanced at the hands of the clock every now and then with as much impatience as human judges who, in session since morning, cannot keep from dreaming of dinner, of their family, and of their beloved slippers. If there is some haste and chance in supernatural justice, don't be surprised that human justice is sometimes similar. We ourselves would be, in that case, unjust judges.

So that day a few blunders were committed which might seem weird, if prudence, rather than caprice, were the Fairies' distinctive, eternal trait.

So the power magnetically to attract wealth was decreed to the sole heir of a very rich family, who, not gifted with a sense of charity, nor even any greed for life's most visible goods, would later find himself prodigiously encumbered by his millions.

So a love for Beauty and Poetic Power were given to the son of a sullen pauper, quarryman by trade, who could not, in any way, assist the faculties, nor alleviate the needs of his pitiable progeny.

I forgot to tell you that the distribution, on those solemn occasions, is without appeal, and that no gift can be refused.

While all the Fairies were rising, believing their drudgery finished—for no gift remained, no liberality to throw to the human small fry—a fine fellow got up, a pitiful little merchant, I believe, and, grabbing the Fairy closest to him by her robe of multicolored vapors, shouted:

"What, Madam! you are forgetting us! My little one is still here! I don't want to have come for nothing."

The Fairy could have been flustered; for there remained *nothing*. However, just in time she remembered a law, well known although rarely applied in the supernatural world, inhabited by those intangible deities, friends of mankind, such as Fairies, Gnomes, Salamanders, Sylphids, Sylphs, Nixies, male and female water sprites—I mean the law which concedes to Fairies, in cases similar to this one, that is, when shares run out, the ability to give still another, additional and exceptional one, provided, however, that she has enough imagination to create it immediately.

So the good Fairy replied, with a self-assurance worthy of her rank: "I give to your son... I give him... the *Gift of Pleasing!*"

"But to please how? Pleasing?... Why pleasing?" doggedly asked the little shopkeeper, who was probably one of those all too common rationalizers, unable to elevate themselves to the logic of the Absurd.

"Because! Because!" answered the enraged Fairy, turning her back on him. And she returned to the procession of her companions, saying: "What do you think of that vain little Frenchman, who wants to understand everything, and who, having acquired the best share for his son, still dares to question and to dispute the indisputable?"

# THE TEMPTATIONS,
# OR EROS, PLUTUS, AND FAME

Last night, two magnificent Satans and a no less extraordinary She-Devil climbed the mysterious staircase through which Hell assaults the weakness of sleeping people and secretely communicates with them. And they posed arrogantly before me, as if standing on a platform. A sulfurous splendor emanated from these three characters, who thus stood out against the night's dark backdrop. They appeared so proud and so full of domination that at first I took all three for real Gods.

The first Satan's face was of an ambiguous sex, and also, his body's contours had some of the limpness of a Bacchus of antiquity. His lovely, languid dark eyes, of undefined color, resembled violets still weighed down with a storm's heavy tears, and his parted lips warm incense burners, from which a fine perfumed odor emanated; and each time he sighed, musky insects, flitting about, would light up in his burning breath.

A shimmering snake was wrapped like a belt around his purple tunic and, raising its head, languorously directed its fiery eyes on him. On that living belt, alternating with vials filled with ominous liquors, were suspended shiny knives and surgical instruments. In his right hand he held another vial with luminous red contents, and which bore these weird words as a label: "Drink, this is my blood, a perfect remedy." His left hand held a violin which probably helped him sing his pleasures and sorrows, spreading the contagion of his madness during witches' sabbath nights.

Delacroix pinx¹ et lith.  Ch. Motte, Imp. Lith. à Paris

Faust.___ Ma belle Demoiselle, oserois-je vous offrir mon bras et vous reconduire chez vous

At his delicate ankles hung a few links of a broken gold chain, and when the resulting discomfort forced him to lower his eyes toward the ground, he conceitedly contemplated his toenails, shiny and polished like well-wrought gems.

He looked at me with his inconsolably woeful eyes, from which flowed an insidious intoxication, and he said to me in a singsong voice, "If you want, if you want, I will make you the lord of souls, and you will be the master of living matter, even more than the sculptor masters clay. And you will experience the pleasure, ceaselessly reborn, of leaving yourself so as to forget yourself in others, and of attracting other souls until you absorb them into yours."

And I replied, "Thanks a lot! I want nothing to do with those shoddy creatures who, probably, are not worth more than my pitiful self. Although I'm sometimes ashamed to recollect, I don't want to forget anything. And even if I didn't know you, old monster, your mysterious cutlery, your equivocal vials, the chains entangling your feet, are symbols which explain clearly enough the drawbacks of your friendship. Keep your presents."

The second Satan had neither that tragic and smiling manner, nor those lovely ingratiating mannerisms, nor that delicate and perfumed beauty. He was a huge man, with a fat eyeless face, whose massive potbelly sagged over his hips, and his whole hide was gilded and decorated, like tattooing, with an array of little moving figures representing the myriad forms of universal wretchedness. There were little emaciated men willingly hanging themselves on nails; deformed, skinny little gnomes, whose imploring eyes solicited alms more effectively than their trembling hands; and then aged mothers carrying their misshapen infants hitched onto their withered breasts. There were ever so many more.

The fat Satan thumped his fist on his immense belly, from which emerged a long and reverberating clinking of metal, finishing as a vague groaning formed by many human voices. And, insolently displaying his rotted teeth, he laughed an enormous idiotic laugh, like certain men from all countries when they have overindulged.

And this one told me, "I can give you what buys everything, what is worth everything, what replaces everything!" And he thumped his monstrous belly, whose resonant echo explained his coarse words.

I turned away in disgust, and I replied, "I don't need anyone's wretchedness for my delight; and I don't desire wealth saddened with all the misfortunes pictured, like wallpaper, on your skin."

As for the She-Devil, I would be lying if I didn't admit that at first sight I found in her a weird charm. To define that charm, I could compare it to nothing better than to that of quite beautiful women past their prime, who have stopped aging, however, and whose beauty preserves the penetrating magic of ruins. Her manner was at once haughty and awkward, and her eyes, although wearied, possessed hypnotic power. The mystery in her voice impressed me the most, evoking memories of the most delectable *contralti,* and the slight huskiness of throats constantly washed by brandy.

"Do you want to know my power?" said the false goddess with her charming and paradoxical voice. "Listen!"

And then she placed her lips on a gigantic trumpet, beribboned, like a reed pipe, with headlines from every newspaper in the universe, and, through that trumpet, she shouted my name, which thus crossed the spaces with the noise of a hundred thousand thunderbolts, and returned to me reverberating with an echo from the most distant planet.

"Damn!" I exclaimed, half conquered, "Now that is something precious!" But, examining the seductive virago more carefully, vaguely I thought I recognized her as someone I had seen boozing with some rascals I knew; and the hoarse sound of brass brought to my ears some obscure memory of a prostituted trumpet.

So I replied, with utter contempt, "Get away! I'm not the type to marry the mistress of certain people I don't care to name."

For sure, I had the right to be proud of such courageous self-denial. But unfortunately I woke up, and all my strength abandoned me. "Really," I said to myself, "I must've been quite deeply asleep to display such scruples. Ah! If only they could come back while I'm awake, I wouldn't be so fussy!"

And I appealed out loud, entreating them to forgive me, offering to dishonor myself as often as necessary to earn their favors. But I had probably offended them quite badly, for they never returned.

# 22

# TWILIGHT

Daylight falls. A great calming forms in pitiable minds wearied by the day's toil; and their thoughts now absorb twilight's tender and indistinct tints.

Meanwhile a great howling, composed of a multitude of discordant shouts, reaches my balcony from the mountaintop, through the evening's transparent clouds, and transformed by the space into a dismal harmony, like a rising tide or an awakening storm.

Who are the hapless ones not calmed by evening, and who, like owls, take the night's arrival as a sign of witches' sabbath? Their ominous ululation reaches us from the dark asylum perched on the mountain. And in the evening, when the wind blows from above, I can lull my mind astonished at this imitation of hell's harmonies, smoking and contemplating the stillness of the immense valley which bristles with houses whose every window says, "Here is peace, here is family joy!"

Twilight agitates madmen. —I remember two of my friends whom twilight would make quite ill. The first one would then neglect all friendly and polite ties, and abuse the first-comer, like a savage. I saw him throw an excellent chicken, which he believed to be some insulting hieroglyph, at a headwaiter's face. The evening, herald of profound voluptuous pleasures, spoiled the most succulent things for him.

The other one, wounded in his ambition, would become more bitter, gloomier, more pestering as daylight faded. Still kindly and sociable by day, in the evening he was merciless; and not only others, but also he himself bore the brunt of his furious twilight madness.

The first one died insane, unable to recognize his wife and child. The second carries within himself the anxiety of a perpetual disquiet; and, even were he rewarded with every honor republics and princes can confer, I think that twilight would still rekindle his burning desire for imaginary distinctions.

Night, which puts its darkness into their minds, illumines mine; and, although it is not unusual to see the same cause beget two opposite effects, it always intrigues and alarms me.

O night! O refreshing darkness! For me you signal an inward celebration, you are the liberation from anguish! In the solitude of the plains, amidst the stony labyrinths of a capital, sparkling with stars, explosion of street lamps, you are the fireworks of the goddess Liberty!

Twilight, how gentle and tender you are! The pink glows still lingering on the horizon like the day dying under its night's victorious subjugation, the fires of candelabra forming spots of opaque red on the sunset's final glories, the heavy draperies drawn by an invisible hand from the depths of the East, imitate all the complicated feelings struggling in a person's heart during life's solemn hours.

Or it appears like a strange dancing dress, whose transparent and dark gauze reveals a glimpse of the muted splendors of a brilliant skirt, just as the delectable past might pierce through the gloomy present. While the trembling gold and silver stars, sprinkled over it, represent those fires of fantasy which ignite well only under the deep mourning of the Night.

# 23

# SOLITUDE

A philanthropic journalist tells me that solitude is bad for people; and to support his thesis, like all unbelievers, he cites sayings of the Church Fathers.

I know that the Demon gladly frequents arid places, and that the Spirit of murder and lechery marvelously flares up in solitudes. But it might also be true that solitude is dangerous only for idle and wandering souls who populate it with their passions and their chimeras.

No question that a chatterbox, whose supreme pleasure consists in speaking from the heights of a pulpit or a forum, would certainly risk going raving mad on Robinson's island. I do not demand of my journalist Crusoe's courageous virtues, but I request that he not bring a charge against lovers of solitude and mystery.

Our jabbering races include individuals who would accept the supreme torture less reluctantly if they were allowed to deliver a copious harangue from the scaffold's heights, without fearing that Santerre's drums might cut their words short at an untimely moment.

I do not pity them, because I suspect that their oratorical outpourings gain them voluptuous pleasures equal to those which others find in silence and meditation. But I despise them.

I especially want my damned journalist to let me enjoy myself as I like. "Then you never feel the need to share your delights?" he says to me, with a very apostolic nasal tone. Look at that subtle envious one! The disgusting spoilsport, he knows that I look down on his, and he comes worming his way into mine!

"That great woe of not being able to be alone!..." La Bruyère says somewhere, perhaps intending to shame everyone who rushes into crowds to forget themselves, probably afraid they couldn't tolerate themselves.

"Almost all our woes come from not being capable of remaining in our rooms," said another wise man, Pascal, I believe, by way of summoning to their meditative cells all the panic-stricken who seek happiness in movement and in a prostitution I could call *fraternitary*, if I would agree to speak the lovely tongue of my century.

# 24

# PLANS

He was saying to himself, walking in a large solitary park, "How beautiful she would be dressed in complicated and sumptuous court apparel, descending a palace's marble steps, opposite large lawns and fountains, in the atmosphere of a lovely evening! For she has the natural bearing of a princess."

Later, roaming down a street, he stopped at an engraving shop, pulled a print depicting a tropical landscape out of a box, and said to himself, "No! I don't want to possess her beloved life in a palace. There we wouldn't be *at home*. Besides, those gold-covered walls would leave no place to hang her likeness; those solemn galleries have no nooks for intimacy. Certainly, *here* is where we must dwell to cultivate the dream of my life."

And so, while his eyes were analyzing the engraving's details, he continued mentally, "At the seashore, a lovely wood cabin, shrouded by all those weird and shiny trees whose names I've forgotten…, in the atmosphere, an intoxicating, undefinable fragrance…, in the cabin a powerful scent of rose and musk…, farther away, behind our little estate, tops of masts rocked by the swell…, around us, beyond the bedroom illumined with pink light filtering through the blinds, decorated with fresh mats and inebriating flowers, with rare Portuguese rococo chairs, made of heavy and dark wood (where she would repose so calm, so well fanned, smoking slightly opiated tobacco!), beyond the veranda, the uproar of birds intoxicated with the light, and the jabbering of little Negresses..., and, at night, lending accompaniment to my dreams, the doleful song of musical trees, of melancholy filaos! Yes, in fact, *that* is the scenery I was looking for. What would I do with a palace?"

And further on, while following a large avenue, he noticed a neat and tidy inn, where two merry heads were leaning out a window enlivened by curtains of gaudy calico. And immediately, he said to himself, "My mind must be quite a vagabond to go looking so far for what is so near me. Pleasure and happiness are at the first inn reached, at the inn of chance, so fertile in voluptuous pleasures. A large fire, garish crockery, a tolerable supper, coarse wine, a very wide bed with sheets a bit rough, but fresh. What could be better?"

And returning home alone, at that hour when Wisdom's advice is no longer stifled by the buzzings of the exterior life, he said to himself, "Today, in dream, I had three domiciles where I found equal pleasure. Why force my body to change location, when my soul travels so nimbly? And what good is it to carry out plans, since planning itself is a sufficient delight?"

# 25

# BEAUTIFUL DOROTHY

The sun overwhelms the city with its direct and fearsome light; the sand is dazzling and the sea shimmers. Stunned people slackly collapse and take a siesta, a siesta which is a sort of delectable death where the sleeper, half-awake, relishes the voluptuous pleasures of his annihilation.

Meanwhile Dorothy, strong and proud like the sun, advances down the deserted street, at that moment the only one alive under the boundless azure, and forming a spot brilliant and black against the light.

She advances, languidly swaying her so slender torso on her hips so broad. Her dress of clinging silk, light-colored and pink, vividly stands out against her skin's darkness and molds her tall figure, her furrowed back, and pointed breasts exactly.

Her red parasol, filtering the light, casts the bloody rouge of its reflections onto her dark face.

The weight of her enormous, almost blue tresses bends her delicate head backward and makes it seem triumphal and lazy. Heavy earrings warble mysteriously at her pretty ears.

Now and then the sea breeze lifts the corner of her flowing skirt and displays her gleaming and magnificent legs. And, like the feet of marble goddesses incarcerated in European museums, her feet faithfully imprint their form in the powdery sand. Since Dorothy is so enormously alluring, her pleasure at being admired prevails over her pride at being a freed slave, and, although she is free, she walks shoeless.

She advances thus, harmoniously, happy to live and smil-

Dessin de
Baudelaire.
27 fev.
1865

quærens
quem
devoret.

ing a vacant smile, as if glancing at a mirror in the distant space reflecting her gait and her beauty.

At the hour when even dogs whine with pain under the biting sun, what great purpose makes lazy Dorothy venture thus, beautiful and cold as bronze?

Why has she left her little hut, so attractively kept, whose flowers and mats make a perfect boudoir at such little cost; where she takes such pleasure combing herself, smoking, being fanned or looking at herself in the mirror of her huge feathered fans? While the sea, striking the beach a hundred feet away, lends a powerful and monotonous accompaniment to her vague reveries, and her iron pot, simmering a crab stew with rice and saffron, from the back courtyard, sends her its arousing aromas.

Perhaps she has a date with some young officer, who has heard his comrades, on distant beaches, talk about the famous Dorothy. The simple creature, inevitably, will beseech him to describe balls at the Opera House, and ask if you can go barefoot there, like at Sunday dances, where even the old Kaffir women get drunk and raging with joy. And still again, if all the beautiful Parisian ladies are more beautiful than she.

Dorothy is admired and pampered by everyone, and she would be perfectly happy if she were not duty bound to save up piastre by piastre in order to ransom her little sister who is indeed eleven years old, and already ripe, and so beautiful! She will probably succeed, good Dorothy. The child's master is so miserly, too miserly to understand any beauty other than that of cash!

# 26

# THE EYES OF THE POOR

Ah, you want to know why I hate you today! It will probably be less easy for you to understand why than for me to explain; for you are, I believe, the most beautiful example of feminine impermeability anyone can meet.

We had spent a long day together which seemed short to me. We had indeed promised each other that all our thoughts would be shared with each other, and that our two souls would henceforth form but one. —Anyway, there is nothing original about this dream, except that, dreamed by everyone, no one has fulfilled it.

In the evening, you were a bit tired and wanted to sit at a brand-new café on the corner of a new boulevard, still full of debris and already ostentatiously exhibiting its unfinished splendors. The café was sparkling. Even its gas lights displayed all the fervor of an opening, and at full blast they illumined the blindingly white walls, the mirrors' dazzling expanses, the gilding of the moldings and cornices, the chubby-cheeked pages dragged about by leashed dogs, the ladies laughing at the falcon perched on their fist, the nymphs and goddesses carrying fruits, pâtés, and game on their heads, the Hebes and Ganymedes presenting with outstretched arms little amphoras of mousse or bicolored obelisks of blended ice creams. All history and all mythology at the command of gluttony.

On the street, right in front of us, was planted a good fellow about forty years old, with a tired face, a graying beard, holding a little boy with one hand and carrying on his other arm a little creature too weak to walk. He was filling the charge of nursemaid and taking his children out in the evening air. Everyone in tatters. Those three faces were extraordinarily serious, and those six eyes fixedly contemplated the brand-new café with equal admiration, but variously nuanced by their ages.

The father's eyes were saying, "How beautiful! How beautiful! All the poor world's gold seems to have fallen upon these walls." —The little boy's eyes, "How beautiful! How beautiful! But only people not like us can enter this house." As for the eyes of the smallest, they were too hypnotized to express anything other than stupefied and deep joy.

Popular singers say that pleasure makes the soul kind and softens the heart. The song was right that evening, relative to me. Not only was I moved by that family of eyes, but I felt a little ashamed of our glasses and decanters, larger than our thirst. I turned my gaze toward yours, dear love, in order to read *my* thought there. As I was plunging into your eyes so beautiful and so weirdly soft, into your green eyes, the abode of Caprice and inspired by the Moon, you said, "I can't stand those people with their eyes wide open like entrance gates! Can't you ask the headwaiter to send them away?"

How difficult it is to understand one another, my dear angel, and how uncommunicable thought is, even among people who love each other!

# 27

# A HEROIC DEATH

Fanciullo was an admirable buffoon, and almost one of the Prince's friends. But serious matters have a fatal attraction for people whose state destines them to the comical, and, although it might seem odd that the ideas of fatherland and freedom can despotically seize a playactor's brain, one day Fancioulle entered into a conspiracy formed by some disgruntled gentlemen.

Everywhere there exist decent people who denounce to the authorities those hot-tempered individuals who try to depose princes and to operate, without consulting it, the dismantling of a society. The lords in question were arrested, as was Fanciullo, and destined to certain death.

I readily believe that the Prince was almost angry to find his favorite actor among the rebels. The Prince was neither better nor worse than anyone else; but his excessive sensitivity made him, in many instances, crueler and more despotic than all his peers. Passionately enamored of the fine arts, moreover an excellent connoisseur, he was truly insatiable for voluptuous pleasures. Himself a true artist, rather indifferent toward people and morality, he recognized but one dangerous enemy, Ennui, and the weird efforts he made to flee or to conquer that tyrant of the world would certainly have won him, from a severe historian, the epithet of "monster," had he been allowed to write anything whatever, on such matters, not exclusively associated with pleasure or astonishment, which is one of pleasure's most delicate forms. It was the Prince's great misfortune never to have a theater vast enough for his genius. Some young Neros do exist who stifle within too narrow limits, and whose names and goodness future centuries will never know. A heedless Providence had given this one faculties greater than his States.

Suddenly the rumor circulated that the sovereign wanted to pardon all the conspirators. And the source of that rumor was the announcement of a great performance in which Fanciullo was to play one of his major and most successful roles, and which even the condemned gentlemen, it was said, would attend. An obvious sign, added the superficial minds, of the offended Prince's generous leanings.

Everything was possible from such a naturally and willfully eccentric man, even virtue, even clemency, especially if he hoped it would give him unexpected pleasures. But for those who, like myself, could probe more deeply into that curious and sick soul, it was infinitely more probable that the Prince intended to evaluate the theatrical talents of a man condemned to death. He wanted to profit from the opportunity of making a physiological experiment of *capital* interest, and to verify to what extent an artist's normal faculties can be changed or modified by his extraordinary situation. Beyond that, did there lie within his soul a more or less defined intention of clemency? That point could never be clarified.

Finally, the great day reached, that little court displayed all its magnificence, and, unless you had seen them, it would be hard to conceive all the splendors that the privileged class of a little State, with restricted resources, could exhibit for a true solemn occasion. This one was doubly so, first for the magic of its flaunted excess, then for the psychological and mysterious interest associated with it.

Seigneur Fanciullo particularly excelled in silent roles or ones burdened with few words, often the major roles in fairy dramas depicting symbolically the mystery of life. He came out onto the stage smoothly and perfectly at ease, which contributed to reinforcing, amongst the noble public, the idea of mildness and pardon.

When it is said of an actor, "What a good actor," the expression implies that the actor can still be glimpsed beneath the character, that is to say, art, effort, will. Now, if an actor should succeed in being, relative to the character he is assigned to portray, what the best statues of antiquity, if miraculously animated, living, walking, seeing, might become relative to the general and vague idea of beauty, it would be, probably, a unique and completely unexpected event. That evening, Fanciullo was a perfect idealization, impossible not to imagine as living, possible, real. The buffoon went, came, laughed, wept, contorted himself, with an indestructible halo around his head, a halo invisible to everyone, but visible to me, and in which were blended, in a strange amalgam, the rays of Art and the glory of Martyrdom. By what special grace I know not, Fanciullo infused the divine and the supernatural, even into his most extravagant buffooneries. My pen trembles, and tears of a still-present emotion fill my eyes as I try to describe that unforgettable evening. Fanciullo proved to me, in a peremptory, irrefutable way, that the intoxication of Art is more apt than any other to veil the terrors of the abyss; that genius can play comedy on the brink of death with a joy that keeps it from seeing the tomb, lost, as it is, in a paradise excluding any idea of tomb and destruction.

The whole audience, as jaded and frivolous as could be, soon yielded to the artist's all-powerful domination. No one dreamed any longer of death, of mourning, nor of torture. Everyone succumbed, without fear, to the multiplied voluptuous pleasures bestowed by the sight of a masterpiece of living art. Explosions of joy and admiration time and again shook the vaults of the edifice with the force of constant thunder. Even the Prince, intoxicated, mingled his applause with that of his court.

However, for a discerning eye, his intoxication, his own, was not unmixed. Did he feel defeated in his despotic power? humiliated in his art of terrifying hearts and numbing minds? frustrated in his hopes and mocked in his predictions? Such assumptions, not exactly justified, but not absolutely unjustifiable, crossed my mind as I was contemplating the Prince's face, upon which a new pallor continuously increased his usual pallor, like snow added to snow. His lips tightened more and more, and his eyes shone with an inner fire like jealousy and spite, even while he was conspicuously applauding the talents of his old friend, the strange buffoon, who was playing death's buffoon so well. At a certain point, I saw His Highness lean toward a little page, stationed behind him, and speak into his ear. The pretty child's mischievous physiognomy lit up with a smile; and then he swiftly left the princely circle, as if to run an urgent errand.

A few minutes later a shrill, drawn-out whistle blast interrupted Fanciullo at one of his greatest moments, and shattered both ears and hearts. And from the place in the theater where that unexpected disapproval had burst forth, a child rushed into a corridor with muffled laughter.

Fanciullo, jolted, awakened from within his dream, first closed his eyes, then opened them almost immediately, enormously enlarged, then opened his mouth as though convulsively breathing, staggered a little forward, a little backward, and then fell stone dead upon the stage.

Had the whistle, swift as a sword, really thwarted the executioner? Had the Prince himself suspected the homicidal efficiency of his trick? There is ground to doubt it. Was he sorry about his dear and inimitable Fanciullo? It is sweet and legitimate to believe so.

The guilty gentlemen had enjoyed a comic spectacle for the last time. That very night they were erased from life.

Since then, several mimes, justly appreciated in different

lands, have come to play for the court of ——; but none of them could duplicate the marvelous talents of Fanciullo, nor rise to the same *favor*.

# 28

# THE COUNTERFEIT COIN

As we were leaving the tobacco shop, my friend made a careful sorting of his change. In the left pocket of his vest he slipped some little gold coins; in the right, some little silver coins; in the left pocket of his trousers, a load of thick pennies, and finally, in the right, a silver two-franc coin he had examined particularly well.

"Peculiar and meticulous allocation!" I said to myself.

We encountered a poor man who held out his cap to us, trembling. —I know of nothing more upsetting than the mute eloquence of those beseeching eyes, containing at one and the same time, for the sensitive man who can read them, such humility, such reproaches. There he finds something close to the depth of complex feeling, in the tearful eyes of dogs being whipped.

My friend's offering was much more substantial than mine, and I told him, "You're right. After the pleasure of being astonished, there's none greater than making a surprise."

"That was the counterfeit coin," he replied calmly, as if to defend his prodigality.

But into my miserable brain, always busy finding complications (what a tiresome faculty nature bestowed upon me!), the idea suddenly came that such an action, on my friend's part, might be excusable only by his desire to create an event in that poor devil's life, perhaps even to learn about the various consequences, harmful or not, that a false coin in a beggar's hands might produce. Might it not multiply into real coins? Might it not also lead him to prison? A tavern keeper, a baker, for example, might have him arrested as a counterfeiter or a propagator of counterfeit coins. Or the false coin could just as well become, for a poor little speculator, the seed of a few days' wealth. And thus my fancy went its way, lending its wings to my friend's mind and drawing all possible deductions from all possible hypotheses.

But he abruptly shattered my reverie by repeating my own words, "Yes, you're right. There's no sweeter pleasure than surprising a man by giving him more than he hopes for."

I looked him straight in the eye, and I was appalled to see his eyes shining with unquestionable candor. Then I understood clearly that he had tried at one and the same time to accomplish an act of charity and a good deal; to earn forty pennies and God's heart; to carry off paradise economically; finally, to snatch gratis his certificate as a charitable man.

I might almost have forgiven his desire for the criminal delight of which I had just assumed him capable. I might have found it curious, unique, that he would enjoy compromising poor people; but I will never forgive him for the incompetence of his calculation.

It is never excusable to be mean, but there is some merit in knowing that you are; and the most irreparable of vices is to do evil through stupidity.

# 29

# THE GENEROUS GAMBLER

Yesterday, amidst the boulevard crowd, I felt brush against me a mysterious Being I had always desired to meet, and whom I immediately recognized, although I had never seen him. He probably felt an analogous desire, for, in passing, he gave me a meaningful wink I hastened to obey.

I carefully followed him, and promptly went behind him into an underground dwelling, dazzling, far more extravagant than the most eminent Parisian residences. It seemed remarkable that I could have passed by that prestigious lair so often without divining its entrance.

An exquisite, though inebriating atmosphere reigned there, which almost instantaneously made one forget all life's tedious horrors. There you breathed a dismal beatitude, similar to what the lotus-eaters must have experienced when they landed on an enchanted island, illumined with the glows of an eternal afternoon, and, hearing the soporific sounds of melodious waterfalls, felt quicken within them a desire never again to see their domestic gods, their wives, their children, and never again to embark upon the sea's high waves.

There were strange faces of men and women, marked with a fatal beauty, which I might have already seen at times and in lands impossible for me to recall exactly, and which aroused my brotherly sympathy rather than that fear usually provoked by the sight of the unknown. To attempt somehow to define the unique expression of their gaze, I might say that never have I seen eyes shining more forcefully with a

De temps en temps j'aime à voir le vieux Père,
Et je me garde bien de lui rompre en visière.

dread of ennui and an immortal desire to feel themselves live.

My host and I, by the time we sat down, had already become familiar and fast friends. We ate, we drank immoderately all kinds of extraordinary wines, and, what was no less extraordinary, after several hours it seemed that I was no more drunk than he.

Gambling, however, that superhuman pleasure, at different intervals interrupted our frequent libations, and I admit that I gambled and lost my soul, winner take all, with heroic carelessness and frivolity.

The soul is such an impalpable thing, so often useless and sometimes such a nuisance, that I experienced only a little less fright at that loss, than as if, during a walk, I had misplaced my calling card.

We lingered smoking some cigars whose incomparable taste and aroma made my soul yearn for lands and happiness unknown, and, intoxicated with all these delights, in a burst of familiarity which seemed not to displease him, grabbing a goblet full to the brim I boldly exclaimed, "To your immortal health, old Goat!"

We also chatted about the universe, its creation and its future destruction; about the century's great idea, that is, of progress and perfectability, and, in general, about every kind of human self-conceit.

On that particular subject, His Highness never ran out of frivolous and irrefutable jokes, and he expressed himself with a smoothness of diction and calm humor I have not seen in mankind's most famous conversationalists.

He demonstrated the absurdity of different philosophies which had possessed the human brain until now, and he even condescended to entrust me with some basic principles whose profits and possession I should not share in any way with anyone. He did not complain at all about the bad reputation he enjoys throughout the world. He maintained that he himself was the person most desirous of destroying *super-stition*, and admitted that only once had he feared for his own power, the day he heard a preacher, more discerning than his colleagues, shout from the pulpit, "My dear brothers, when you hear the progress of enlightenment extolled, never forget that the devil's cleverest trick is to persuade you that he does not exist!"

Recalling that famous orator naturally led us to the subject of academies, and my strange table-companion asserted that, in many cases, it was not beneath him to inspire the pen, the words and the conscience of pedagogues, and that he almost always attended in person, although invisible, every academy session.

Encouraged by so many benefits, I asked him for some news of God, and if he had seen him recently. He replied, with a nonchalance nuanced by a certain sadness, "We greet each other when we meet, but like two old gentlemen whose innate civility cannot completely extinguish the memory of old grudges."

I doubt that His Highness has ever given such a long audience to a simple mortal, and I was afraid to impose.

Finally, as the trembling dawn whitened the windows, this famous character, sung by so many poets and served by so many philosophers working for his glory unaware, told me: "I want you to remember well of me and to prove that I Myself, so ill-spoken of, am sometimes a *good devil*, to use one of your popular expressions. So, to compensate the irremediable loss of your soul, I give you the stake you would have won if fate was on your side, namely the possibility of alleviating and conquering, for your entire life, that weird ailment Ennui, the source of all your ills and all your wretched progress. Never will you form a desire I will not help you to fulfill. You will rule over your vulgar peers. You will be provided with flattery and even adoration. Silver, gold, diamonds, fairy palaces, will pursue you and beg you to accept them, without your exerting any effort to earn them. You will change fatherland and region as often as your fancy dictates. You will carouse in voluptuous pleasures, without weariness, in enchanting lands where it is always warm and where women smell as good as flowers—et cetera, et cetera...," he added, getting up and dismissing me with a nice smile.

If I hadn't been afraid to disgrace myself before such a distinguished convocation, I would gladly have fallen at that generous gambler's feet, to thank him for his incredible munificence. But after I left him, incurable distrust gradually returned to my bosom. I no longer dared to believe in such prodigious good fortune, and, going to bed, still saying my prayers as part of an idiotic habit, I repeated, half-asleep, "My God! Lord, my God! Make the devil keep his promise!"

# THE ROPE

*To Edouard Manet*

"Illusions," my friend was telling me, "are perhaps as countless as relationships between people, or between people and things. And when the illusion disappears, that is, when we perceive the creature or the fact such as it exists outside of us, we experience a weird feeling, complicated half with regret for the vanished phantom, half with pleasant surprise at the novelty, the real fact. If any phenomenon is obvious, trite, constantly the same, and whose nature it is impossible to misunderstand, it is motherly love. It is as hard to presume a mother to be without motherly love than a light without heat. So therefore, is it not perfectly legitimate to ascribe to motherly love all a mother's actions and words, relative to her child? And yet listen to this little story of how I was remarkably duped by the most natural illusion.

"My profession as a painter prompts me attentively to examine faces, physiognomies, turning up on my path, and you know what delight we gain from that faculty which makes life appear more lively and more meaningful to us than to other people. In the remote neighborhood where I live, and with vast grass-grown spaces still between the buildings, I often watched a child whose fervent and mischievous physiognomy, more than any others, immediately seduced me. He posed for me more than once, and I sometimes transformed him into a little gypsy, sometimes into an angel, sometimes into a mythological Cupid. I had him carry a vagabond's violin, the Crown of Thorns and Nails of the Passion, and the torch of Eros. At last that kid's every whimsy gave me such lively pleasure that one day I asked his parents, poor people, if they would agree to hand him over to me, promising to dress him well, give him money, and not to impose any hardship other than cleaning my brushes and running my errands. The child, washed up, became charming, and he thought the life he led at my house was a paradise, compared to what he would have endured in the paternal hovel. But I admit that the little fellow sometimes surprised me with peculiar fits of precocious sadness, and that he soon showed an immoderate craving for sugar and liquors. So that one day, confirming that he had again committed another such theft, despite my many warnings, I threatened to return him to his parents. Then I went out, and my business kept me away from home for a fairly long time.

"Imagine my horror and astonishment when, back home, the first object that struck my gaze was my little fellow, the mischievous companion of my life, hanging from the paneling of that wardrobe! His feet almost touched the floor; a chair, which he had probably pushed with his foot, was overturned beside him; his head tilted convulsively toward one shoulder; his bloated face, and his eyes, wide open in a frightful stare, at first produced the illusion of life. Taking him down was not as easy a task as you might believe. He was already quite stiff, and I was inexplicably reluctant to let him drop abruptly to the ground. I had to support his whole body with one arm, and, with the hand of the other arm, cut the rope. But that being done, everything was not finished. The little monster had used very fine twine which had entered deeply into the flesh, and in order to release it from the neck, with fine scissors, I now had to locate the rope between the two folds of the swelling.

"I didn't tell you that I had vigorously called for help. But all my neighbors refused to come help me, faithful in that way to the habits of civilized people who, I don't know why, never want to get involved in the business of a hanged person. A doctor finally arrived and declared that the child had been dead for several hours. Later, when we had to undress him for the burial, his cadaverous stiffness was such that we gave up trying to move his limbs and had to rip and cut his clothes in order to remove them.

"The Police inspector, to whom, naturally, I had to report the accident, looked at me askance, and said, 'Something is shady here!' probably moved by the inveterate wish and professional habit of intimidating, quite randomly, innocent as well as guilty people.

"A supreme task remained to fulfill, the very thought of which caused me frightful anguish: the parents had to be informed. My feet refused to take me there. Finally I got up the courage. But, to my great astonishment, the mother was indifferent, not one tear oozed from the corner of her eye. I attributed that strangeness to the very horror she must be feeling, and I remembered the well-known saying, 'The deepest griefs are silent.' As for the father, he was content to say in a half-stupefied, half-dreamy manner, 'After all, it's probably better this way. He still would've come to a bad end!'

"While the body was lying on my couch, and, helped by a servant woman, I was attending to the final preparations, the mother entered my studio. She wanted, she claimed, to see her son's corpse. I could not, in fact, stop her from intoxicating herself on her misfortune and refuse her that supreme and somber consolation.

Then she requested me to show her the place where her little one had hanged himself. 'Oh no Madam!' I answered her, 'that would upset you.' And while my eyes were turning involuntarily to the funereal wardrobe, I noticed, with disgust mixed with horror and anger, that the nail was still stuck in the paneling, with a long piece of rope still hanging from it. I vigorously rushed to tear away those last vestiges of the misfortune, and just as I began to throw them out the open window, the poor woman grabbed my arm and said with an irresistible voice, 'Oh Sir! Let me have that! Please! I beg of you!' Probably, it seemed to me, that her despair had so crazed her that she was now tenderly enamored of what had been the instrument of her son's death, and she wanted to keep it as a horrible and cherished relic. —So she seized the nail and the string.

"Finally! Finally! Everything was finished. I had only to get back to work, still more vigorously than usual, so as to gradually drive away the little corpse haunting the folds of my brain, and whose phantom irked me with its large staring eyes. But the next day I received a stack of letters: some from tenants in my house, a few others from neighboring homes; one, from the second floor; another, from the third; still another, from the fourth, and so on. Some in a half-jesting style, attempting to disguise the sincerity of their request under an apparent banter; others, clumsily shame-less and badly spelled, but every one aiming toward the same goal, namely, to obtain from me a piece of the deadly and beatific rope. Among the signers, I must admit, there were more women than men; but, believe me, all of them did not belong to the lowly and common class. I kept those letters.

"And then, suddenly, a light went on in my brain, and I understood why the mother was so eager to grab the string from me and by what sort of trade she meant to console herself."

# VOCATIONS

In a beautiful garden where the rays of an autumn sun seemed pleasantly to linger, under an already greenish sky where clouds of gold drifted like traveling continents, four beautiful children, four boys, probably weary of playing, were chatting with each other.

One was saying, "Yesterday I was taken to the theater. In huge and sad palaces, with the sea and sky in the background, men and women, also serious and sad, but much more beautiful and much better dressed than those we see anywhere, speak in melodious voices. They threaten each other, they beg, they are upset, and they often grip a dagger thrust in their belts. Ah! it's so beautiful! The women are much more beautiful and much taller than those who visit us at home, and, though their large hollow eyes and blazing cheeks make them look terrifying, you can't help loving them. You're frightened, you want to cry, and yet you're happy... And then, even more amazing, it makes you want to dress the same way, to say and do the same things, and to speak in the same voice..."

One of the four children, who a few seconds before had stopped listening to his companion's speech and was staring somewhere in the sky with astonishing steadiness, suddenly said, "Look, look over there...! Do you see *him?* He's seated on that little solitary cloud, that little fire-colored cloud, traveling slowly. *He* too, it seems that *he* is looking at us."

"But who is it?" asked the others.

"God!" he replied with a perfect ring of conviction. "Ah! He's already quite distant; soon you'll no longer be able to

see him. He's probably traveling, to visit every country. Wait, he's about to pass behind that row of trees almost touching the horizon... and now he's descending behind the steeple... Ah! he's no longer visible!" And for a long time the child remained turned to the same side, staring at the line separating earth from sky, his eyes glowing with an inexpressible expression of ecstasy and regret.

"That guy is really stupid, with his dear Lord only he can see!" added the third, whose entire little person gave off a remarkable vivaciousness and vitality. "Me, I'm going to tell you how something happened to me which never happened to you, and is a bit more interesting than your theater and your clouds. —A few days ago, my parents took me along on a trip, and, since there were not enough beds for all of us at the inn where we stopped, they decided I would sleep in the same bed as my maid." —He drew his friends closer, and spoke in a hushed voice. "You see, it's amazingly impressive not to sleep alone and to be in bed with your maid, in the darkness. Since I couldn't sleep, I entertained myself, while she was sleeping, by running my hand over her arms, her neck and her shoulders. Her arms and neck are much bigger than any other woman's, and the skin so soft, so soft, it seems like writing paper or tissue paper. I enjoyed it so much that I would've continued for a long time, if I hadn't become frightened, afraid first of awakening her, and then even more afraid of I don't know what. Then I shoved my head into the hair hanging down her back, thick as a mane, and it smelled as good, I assure you, as the garden flowers, right now. When you can, try it too, and you'll see!"

The eyes of the young author of that prodigious revelation, while he told his story, opened wide with some sort of stupefaction at what he was still experiencing, and the rays of the setting sun, slipping through the red curls of his disheveled hair, lit them up like a sulfurous halo of passion. It was easy to guess that he would not waste his life seeking the Divinity in clouds, and that he would frequently find it elsewhere.

Finally the fourth one said: "You know that I have hardly any fun at home; I'm never taken to plays; my guardian is too stingy; God doesn't bother with me and my ennui, and I don't have a beautiful maid to coddle me. I've often thought that my pleasure would be to travel continuously straight ahead, without knowing where, without anyone bothering about it, and always to see new lands. I'm never at ease anywhere, and I always believe I'd feel better anywhere else than where I am. Well! At the last fair of the neighboring village, I found three men who live as I'd like to live. You didn't notice them, you guys. They were tall, almost black and very proud, although in tatters, appearing to need no one. Their big dark eyes shone completely when they made music; a music so surprising that sometimes it makes you want to dance, other times to cry, or to do both at once, and you might almost go crazy if you listened to them too long. One, trailing his bow over his violin, seemed to relate a sorrow, and the other, making his little hammer skip over the strings of a little piano strapped to his neck, appeared to poke fun at his neighbor's lament, while the third, from time to time, would strike his cymbals with extraordinary violence. They were so satisfied with themselves that they kept on playing their wild music, even after the crowd scattered. At the end they picked up their pennies, loaded their baggage onto their backs, and left. As for me, I tried to find out where they lived, followed them from a distance, up to the forest's edge, where I finally understood that they lived nowhere.

"Then one of them said, 'Do we have to pitch the tent?'

"'God no!' the other answered, 'it's such a beautiful night!'

"The third was saying, as he counted their take, 'Music doesn't affect those people, and their women dance like bears. Fortunately, within a month we'll be in Austria, where there'll be a nicer populace.'

"'Perhaps it'd be better to go toward Spain, since the season is almost over. Let's escape and wet only our throats before the rains come,' said one of the other two.

"I remembered it all, as you can see. Then each of them drank a cup of brandy and fell asleep, their brows turned to the stars. At first I wanted to ask them to take me along and teach me how to play their instruments. But I didn't dare, probably because it's always quite hard to make any decision, and also because I'd be caught before getting out of France."

The uninterested attitude of the three other friends made me reflect that this little one was already one of the *misunderstood*. I examined him carefully. There was something or other precociously fatal in his eyes and on his brow which generally repels sympathy, and which, I don't know why, aroused mine, so that for an instant I had the weird thought that I might have a brother to me unknown.

The sun had set. Solemn night had established itself. The children separated, each one going along, unaware, depending on circumstances and chance, to ripen his destiny, to scandalize his peers and gravitate toward fame or toward dishonor.

# 32

# THE THYRSUS

*To Franz Liszt*

What is a thyrsus? According to its social and poetic meaning, it is a sacerdotal emblem to be held by priests and priestesses celebrating the divinity whose interpreters and servants they are. But physically it is only a staff, a mere staff, a vine pole for hops, a vine support, dry, hard, and straight. Around that staff, in capricious meanderings, stems and flowers play and frolic, some sinuous and elusive, others tilted like bells or overturned cups. And an astonishing glory bursts from that complexity of lines and colors, tender or dazzling. Doesn't it seem that the curved and spiral lines are courting the straight line and dance around it in mute adoration? Doesn't it seem that all those delicate corollas, all those calices, explosions of odors and colors, are executing a mystical fandango around the hieratic staff? And yet what foolhardy mortal would dare decide if the flowers and vines were formed for the staff, or if the staff is but the pretext for highlighting the beauty of the vines and flowers?

The thyrsus is the representation of your astonishing duality, powerful and venerable master, dear Bacchant of mysterious and impassioned Beauty. Never did a nymph frenzied by the invincible Bacchus shake her thyrsus over the heads of her crazed companions with as much power and caprice as you wave your genius over your brothers' hearts.

The staff, it is your will, straight, firm, and unshakable; the flowers, the rambling of your fancy around your will; the feminine element executing around the male its prodigious pirouettes. Straight line and arabesque line, intention and expression, tautness of the will, sinuosity of the word, unity of goal, variety of means, all-powerful and indivisible amalgam of genius, what analyst would have the hateful courage to divide and to separate you?

Dear Liszt, through the mists, beyond the rivers, above the cities where pianos celebrate your fame, where printing presses translate your wisdom, in whatever place you may be, in the eternal city's splendors or the mists of the dreamy lands consoled by Gambrinus, improvising songs of delight or of ineffable sorrow, or confiding your abstruse meditations to writing, singer of Voluptuous Pleasure and Anguish eternal, philosopher, poet and artist, I honor you in immortality!

# GET HIGH

You must always be high. Everything depends on it: it is the only question. So as not to feel the horrible burden of Time wrecking your back and bending you to the ground, you must get high without respite.

But on what? On wine, on poetry, or on virtue, whatever you like. But get high.

And if sometimes you wake up, on palace steps, on the green grass of a ditch, in your room's gloomy solitude, your intoxication already waning or gone, ask the wind, the waves, the stars, the birds, clocks, ask everything that flees, everything that moans, everything that moves, everything that sings, everything that speaks, ask what time it is. And the wind, the waves, the stars, the birds, clocks, will answer, "It is time to get high! So as not to be the martyred slaves of Time, get high; get high constantly! On wine, on poetry, or on virtue, as you wish."

# ALREADY!

The sun, radiant or saddened, a hundred times already had burst from that immense vat of the sea whose shores you could hardly distinguish; a hundred times, sparkling or morose, it had again plunged into its boundless bath of evening. For many days, we could contemplate the other side of the firmament and decipher the celestial alphabet of the antipodes. And each passenger would groan and grumble. Approaching land seemed to aggravate their suffering. They said, "When will we ever stop sleeping a sleep jolted by waves, disturbed by wind snoring louder than we? When can we eat meat that isn't salted like the vile element carrying us? When can we digest in an immobile armchair?"

Some of them brooded about their homes, missing their unfaithful and sullen wives, and their screeching progeny. Everyone was so crazed by the image of the absent land, that I think they would have eaten grass more enthusiastically than beasts.

Finally a shoreline was identified. And, drawing near, we saw that it was a magnificent, dazzling land. Life's musics seemed to emerge from it in an indistinct murmur, and its shores, abounding with all varieties of greenery, exuded a delicious odor of flowers and fruits, as far as several leagues.

Everyone suddenly became joyful, everyone relinquished their bad mood. Every quarrel was forgotten, every mutual blame forgiven; arranged duels were blotted from memories, and grudges flew off like smoke.

I alone was sad, inconceivably sad. Like the priest whose

divinity is snatched away, I could not separate myself, without heartbreaking bitterness, from that so monstrously seductive sea, from that sea so infinitely varied in its terrifying simplicity, and which seemed to contain within itself and to represent by its play, its appearances, its angers and its smiles, the moods, the agonies, and the ecstasies of every soul who has lived, who lives and will live!

Saying farewell to that incomparable beauty, I felt depressed unto death. And that is why, when each of my companions said, "Finally!" I could only shout, "*Already!*"

Yet it was land, the land with its sounds, its passions, its conveniences, its festivities. It was a rich and magnificent earth, full of promises, sending us a mysterious aroma of rose and musk, with life's musics reaching us in an amorous murmur.

# WINDOWS

He who looks from the outside through a window open never sees as much as he who looks through a window closed. No deeper, more mysterious, more fertile, more obscure, more dazzling object exists than a window lit by a candle. What you can see in sunlight is always less interesting than what transpires behind a windowpane.

Life lives, life dreams, life suffers in that black or luminous hole.

Beyond the billowing rooftops, I notice a mature woman, already wrinkled, poor, always bent over something, and who never goes out. With her face, her clothing, her gestures, with almost nothing, I have refashioned that woman's history, or rather her legend, and sometimes I tell it to myself weeping.

If it had been a poor old man, I would have just as easily refashioned his as well.

And I go to bed, proud of having lived and suffered in others than myself.

Perhaps you will ask, "Are you sure that legend is the true one?" Does it matter what the reality located outside of me might be, if it has helped me to live, to feel that I am and *what* I am?

# THE DESIRE TO PAINT

Unhappy perhaps the man, but happy the artist shattered by desire!

I burn to paint her who appeared to me so rarely and who fled so quickly, like a beautiful lamented thing left by the traveler swept into the night. She disappeared already so long ago!

She is beautiful, and more than beautiful; she is surprising. Black abounds in her, and everything she inspires is nocturnal and deep. Her eyes are two caves dimly glittering with mystery, and her gaze illumines like lightning: an explosion in the darkness.

I might compare her to a black sun, if you could imagine a black star pouring forth light and happiness. But she reminds you more readily of the moon, which probably branded her with her fearsome influence. Not the white moon of romance, which resembles a frigid bride, but the sinister and intoxicating moon, suspended deep within a stormy night and jostled by fleeing clouds. Not the peaceful and discreet moon attending upon the sleep of pure people, but the moon ripped from the sky, defeated and rebellious, which the Witches of Thessaly fiercely compel to dance on the terrified grass!

A stubborn will and the love of prey dwell on her little brow. However, below her disquieting face, where mobile nostrils inhale the unknown and the impossible, with inexpressible grace, there bursts the laughter of a large mouth, red and white, and delicious, calling to mind the miracle of a magnificent flower budding in volcanic ground.

Some women inspire the need to defeat them and take full pleasure from them; but this one arouses the desire to die slowly under her gaze.

# 37

# THE MOON'S BENEFITS

*To Miss B——*

The Moon, which is caprice itself, looked through the window while you were sleeping in your cradle, and said to herself, "I like that child."

And she unctuously descended her stairway of clouds, and silently passed through the windows. Then she lay on top of you with a mother's agile tenderness, and she placed her colors on your face. So your pupils have remained green, and your cheeks extraordinarily pale. In fact your eyes became so weirdly enlarged by contemplating that visitor. And she grasped your throat so tenderly that you have forever maintained the longing to cry.

Meanwhile the Moon, through her joy's expansion, filled the whole bedroom like a phosphorescent atmosphere, like a luminous poison; and all that living light was thinking and saying, "You will be influenced eternally by my kiss. You will be beautiful the way I am. You will love what I love and what loves me: water, clouds, silence, and night; the sea limitless and green; water shapeless and multiform; places where you will not be; lovers you will not understand; monstrous flowers; aromas that give you delusions; cats fainting on pianos and moaning like women, in a husky and gentle voice.

"And you will be loved by my lovers, courted by my courtiers. You will be the green-eyed queen of men whose throats I also grasped with my nocturnal caresses; of those who love the sea, the limitless sea, tumultuous and green, water shapeless and multiform, places they are not, women they do not understand, sinister flowers resembling censers of an unknown religion, aromas that disturb the will, and wild and voluptuous animals which are the emblems of their madness!"

And that, fiendish dear spoiled child, is why I am now lying at your feet, seeking in your entire person the reflection of the fearsome Divinity, of the fateful stepmother, of the nursemaid poisoner of all *lunatics!*

# WHICH IS THE TRUE ONE?

I met a certain Benedicta, who filled the atmosphere with the ideal, and whose eyes spread the desire for grandeur, beauty, fame, and everything which makes us believe in immortality.

But that miraculous girl was too beautiful to live a long time. So she died a few days after I had made her acquaintance, and it is I myself who buried her, one day when spring was shaking its censer even into the cemeteries. It is I who buried her, tightly sealed into a coffin made of aromatic and rot-proof wood like Indian chests.

And since my eyes were fastened on the place where my treasure was buried, all of a sudden I saw a little person who amazingly resembled the deceased, and who, stamping the fresh soil with a hysterical and weird violence, was saying with bursts of laughter, "It is I, the true Benedicta! It is I, a first-class riffraff! And to punish your madness and your blindness, you will love me as I am!"

But I was furious, and answered, "No! No! No!" And to emphasize my refusal more, I stamped the ground so violently that my leg sank up to the knee in the recent burial place, and so, like a trapped wolf, I remain fettered, perhaps forever, to the grave of the ideal.

# A THOROUGHBRED

She is quite ugly. She is delectable, however!

Time and Love have branded her with their claws and have cruelly taught her what each minute and each kiss subtract from youth and luster.

She is really ugly. She is an ant, a spider, if you wish, even a skeleton; but she is also potion, a balm, witchcraft! All in all, she is exquisite.

Time could not ruin the scintillating harmony of her gait nor the indestructible elegance of her frame. Love has not spoiled the mellowness of her child's breath; and Time has torn nothing from her abundant mane which exudes as musky perfumes all the diabolical vitality of the French South: Nîmes, Aix, Arles, Avignon, Narbonne, Toulouse, cities blessed by the sun, amorous and enchanting!

Time and Love have in vain greedily gnawed on her; they have not diminished the indistinct, but eternal, charm of her boyish breasts.

Deteriorated perhaps, but not wearied, and still heroic, she reminds you of those horses of pure breed recognized by a true connoisseur's eye, even when hitched to a hired coach or a heavy wagon.

And besides she is so gentle and so fervent! She loves as one loves in autumn. Winter's approach seems to light a new fire in her heart, and never is the servility of her tenderness in any way irksome.

# THE MIRROR

A frightful man enters and looks at himself in the mirror.

"Why do you look at yourself in the mirror, since you must see yourself there only with displeasure?"

The frightful man replies, "Sir, according to the immortal principles of '89, all men are by right equal. Thus I possess the right to see my reflection; with pleasure or displeasure, that only concerns my conscience."

According to common sense, I was probably right; but, from the legal viewpoint, he was not wrong.

# THE HARBOR

A harbor is an enchanting abode for souls wearied by life's struggles. The sky's fullness, the mobile architecture of the clouds, the sea's shimmering colorations, the sparkling of lighthouses, are a prism marvelously suited to entertain the eyes without ever tiring them. The slender shapes of boats, with their complicated rigging, to which the swell imparts harmonious rockings, help maintain the soul's craving for rhythm and beauty. And then, especially, there is a sort of mysterious and aristocratic pleasure for someone no longer curious or ambitious enough to contemplate, lying in the belvedere or leaning on the pier, all the movements of those who depart and those who return, of those who still have the strength to will, the desire to travel or to grow rich.

# PORTRAITS OF MISTRESSES

In a man's boudoir, that is, in a smoking room adjoining a fashionable dive, four men were smoking and drinking. They were not exactly young, nor old, nor handsome, nor ugly; but whether old or young, they bore that unmistakable quality of veterans of joy, an indescribable something, a cold and mocking sadness which clearly states, "We have lived intensely and we are seeking something we can love or respect."

One of them steered the conversation to the subject of women. It might have been wiser not to talk about them at all; but some witty people, after drinking, do not despise banal conversations. So they listen to the one talking, as they would listen to dance music.

This one was saying, "All men were once Cherubino's age: that's the stage when, for lack of dryads, you embrace the trunks of oak trees, without distaste. That's love's first step. At the second step, you begin to make choices. Being capable of deliberation is already a decadence. That is when you pursue beauty resolutely. As for me, gentlemen, I'm proud that, already a long time ago, I reached the climacteric age of the third step, when even beauty is not enough if it is not seasoned with perfume, finery, et cetera. I even confess that sometimes I long for a certain fourth step characterized by absolute dispassion, as if it were an unknown happiness. But all my life, except at the Cherubino stage, I've been more vulnerable than anyone to the irritating stupidity, to the exasperating mediocrity of women. What I especially appreciate in animals, is their candor. So

consider how much my last mistress must have made me suffer.

"She was the bastard daughter of a prince. Beautiful, it goes without saying; otherwise, why would I have picked her? But she spoiled that great quality with an unseemly and misshapen ambition. She was a woman who always wanted to play the man's part. 'You're not a man!' 'Ah! if I were a man!' 'Between the two of us, I'm the man!' Such were the unbearable refrains leaving that mouth from which I wished only songs take wing. About a book, a poem, an opera for which I let my admiration slip out, 'Maybe you think that's quite strong?' she'd immediately reply. 'What do you know about strength?' and she would debate.

"One fine day she took up chemistry; so that henceforth I found a mask of glass between my mouth and hers. And besides all that, quite prudish. If sometimes I would perturb her with a slightly too amorous gesture, she would cringe like a ravished flower..."

"How did it end?" said one of the other three. "I didn't know you were so patient."

"God," he continued, "placed the remedy in the evil. One day I found that Minerva, starved for intellectual power, face to face with my servant, and in a position that required me to withdraw discreetly so as not to embarrass them. That evening I dismissed them both, paying them the arrears of their wages."

"As for me," the interrupter went on, "I have only myself to blame. Contentment came to live with me, and I didn't recognize it. Recently Fate accorded me the enjoyment of a woman who was indeed the gentlest, the most submissive and most devoted of creatures, and always available! and without enthusiasm! 'I'm quite willing, since you like it.' That was her usual reply. Give a thrashing to the wall or that couch, and you would draw from it more sighs than outbursts of the most frenzied love would draw from my mistress's breast. After one year of living together, she confessed that she had never enjoyed sex. I got fed up with that unequal duel, and the incomparable girl got married. Later I had the whim to see her again, and she told me, showing me six lovely children, 'Well! my dear friend, the wife is still as much a *virgin* as your mistress was.' Nothing had changed in that person. Sometimes I miss her: I should have married her."

The others began to laugh, and a third one said in turn:

"Gentlemen, I've known delights you have perhaps overlooked. I mean those of the comical in love, and a comical element that does not exclude admiration. I admired my last mistress, I believe, more than you hated or loved yours. And everyone admired her as much as I. When we entered a restaurant, after a few minutes, everyone forgot to eat so as to contemplate her. Even the waiters and the bar lady experienced an ecstasy contagious to the point of forgetting their duties. In brief, for a while I lived in intimacy with a living *phenomenon*. She would eat, chew, grind, devòur, engulf, but in the mildest, most heedless manner. That is how she kept me in ecstasy for a long time. She had a sweet, dreamy, British, and romanesque manner of saying, 'I'm hungry!' And she would repeat those words day and night while showing the prettiest teeth in the world, which would have both touched and amused you. —I might've made my fortune by displaying her at fairs as a *polyphagous monster*. I fed her well, and still she left me..."

"For a caterer, perhaps?"

"Something close, some sort of supply-store employee who, by a stroke of the wand known only to him, probably provided that poor child with the ration of several soldiers. At least that's what I assumed."

"As for me," said the fourth, "I have endured atrocious sufferings from the opposite of what we usually blame selfish females for. I find you to be in a bad position, you all-too-fortunate mortals, to complain about the imperfections of your mistresses!"

That was spoken in a quite serious tone, by a man of gentle and poised appearance, with an almost clerical physiognomy, unhappily lit by light gray eyes, the sort of eyes whose gaze says, "*I want!*" or "*You must!*" or again, "*I never forgive!*"

"If you, as neurotic as I know you to be, G———, as cowardly and superficial as you are, you two, K——— and J———, had been coupled with a certain woman of my acquaintance, either you would have escaped, or you would be dead. Me, I survived, as you see. Imagine a person unable to commit an error of feeling or of calculation. Imagine a devastating serenity of character; devotion without playacting or exaggeration; gentleness without weakness; power without violence. The history of my love resembles an interminable voyage on a surface pure and polished like a mirror, breathtakingly monotonous, which would reflect all my feelings and gestures with the ironic precision of my own conscience. So much that I couldn't yield to an unreasonable gesture or feeling without immediately noticing the silent reproach of my inseparable specter. Love seemed like a guardianship. What follies she prevented me from doing, which I regret not having committed! How many debts repaid in spite of myself! She deprived me of all the profits I might have extracted from my personal madness. With cold and insurmountable rules, she would block all my caprices. Most horrible was that, the danger over, she did not demand any gratitude. So many times I stopped myself from grabbing her by the throat and shouting, 'You wretch! Why aren't you imperfect, so I could love you without anxiety and without anger!' I admired her for several years, my heart filled with hatred. Finally, it was not I who died of it!"

"Ah!" replied the others, "then she died?"

"Yes! It couldn't go on like that. Love had become an overwhelming nightmare for me. Conquer or die, as Politics states, fate forced this choice upon me! One evening, in the woods... at the edge of a pond... after a melancholy walk when her eyes, hers, were reflecting the sky's mildness, and when my heart, mine, was as tense as hell... "

"What?"

"How?"

"What do you mean?"

"It was inevitable. My sense of equity is too strong to strike, to offend or to dismiss an impeccable servant. But I had to reconcile that sense with the horror that creature was arousing in me; eliminate the creature without lacking respect for her. What could you expect me to do, *since she was perfect?*"

The three other companions looked at him with a hazy and slightly dazed look, as if pretending not to understand, and implicitly admitting that, as for themselves, they did not feel capable of such a rigorous action, although otherwise sufficiently justified.

Then they sent for more bottles, to kill Time which has such a resistant life, and to speed up Life, which flows so slowly.

# THE GALLANT MARKSMAN

As the carriage was crossing the woods, he had it stop in the vicinity of a shooting range, saying that it would be enjoyable for him to shoot a few bullets to *kill* Time. Kill that monster, isn't that everyone's most usual and most legitimate pastime? —So he gallantly offered his hand to his dear, delectable, and execrable wife, to that mysterious woman to whom he owed so many pleasures, so many woes, and perhaps also a large part of his genius.

Several bullets hit far from the intended target; one of them even sank into the ceiling. And since the charming creature was laughing madly, mocking her spouse's bad aim, he abruptly turned toward her, and said, "Observe that doll, over there, on the right, sticking its nose in the air and with such a haughty expression. Well dear angel! *I imagine that it is you.*" And he shut his eyes and released the trigger. The doll was cleanly decapitated.

Then bowing to his dear, his delectable, his execrable wife, his inescapable and ruthless Muse, and respectfully kissing her hand, he added, "Ah my dear angel! How I thank you for my aim!"

# THE SOUP AND THE CLOUDS

My little crazy beloved was serving me dinner, and through the dining room's open window I was contemplating the moving architectures that God fashions from vapors, the marvelous constructions of the impalpable. And I was saying to myself, through my contemplation, "All those phantasmagorias are almost as beautiful as the eyes of my beautiful beloved, my little green-eyed monstrous madwoman."

And suddenly I received a violent punch in the back, and I heard a hoarse and charming voice, a hysterical voice and husky as if from brandy, the voice of my dear little beloved, which was saying, "Will you ever eat your soup, you goddamn cloud peddler!"

# THE SHOOTING RANGE
# AND THE CEMETERY

—*Cemetery Vista, Tavern*.

"Strange sign," our stroller said to himself, "but intended to make you thirsty! For certain, that pub's owner appreciates Horace and the poet students of Epicurus. Perhaps he's even familiar with the profound refinement of the ancient Egyptians, who consider no good feast possible without a skeleton, or without some sort of emblem of life's brevity."

And he went in, drank a glass of beer facing the tombs, and slowly smoked a cigar. Then, a whim came over him to go down to that cemetery, whose grass was so high and so inviting, and where such a rich sun held sway.

Indeed, the light and the heat raged there, and the drunken sun seemed to be wallowing stretched out on a carpet of magnificent flowers, fertilized by the decay. A vast buzzing of life filled the air—the life of the infinitely small—which the cracking of gun shots from a neighboring shooting range interrupted at regular intervals, bursting like champagne corks exploding midst the humming of a muted symphony.

Then, the sun heating his brain and in this atmosphere of Death's blazing aromas, he heard a voice whispering under the grave he was sitting on. And that voice said, "Cursed be your targets and your rifles, unruly living ones, who take such little heed of the deceased and their divine repose! Cursed be your ambitions, cursed be your calculations, impatient mortals, who come to study the art of killing near Death's sanctuary! If only you understood how easy it is to win the prize, how easy it is to hit the target, and how everything is nothingness, except Death, you would not wear yourselves out so much, hard-working living ones, and you would less often disturb the sleep of those who have long since reached the Goal, the only true goal of detestable life!"

# LOSS OF HALO

"Hey what! You here, dear fellow! You, in a house of ill fame! You, the drinker of quintessences! You, the ambrosia eater! Really, this takes me by surprise."

"My dear fellow, you know my terror of horses and carriages. Just now, as I was crossing the boulevard, and hopping in the mud, in quite a hurry, through the shifting chaos where death comes galloping from all sides at once, my halo slipped off my head, in one abrupt movement, into the mire of the macadam. I didn't have the guts to pick it up. I considered it less disagreeable to lose my insignia than to break my bones. And anyway, I said to myself, misfortune is good for something. Now I can walk about incognito, commit foul acts, and indulge in debauchery like ordinary mortals. So here I am, just like you, as you can see!"

"At least you should put up a notice for your halo, or have the police advertise for it."

"Good God no! I'm fine here. You're the only one who recognized me. Besides, dignity irks me. And I'm glad to think that some bad poet will pick it up and insolently stick it on his head. Make someone happy, what a delight! and especially a happy someone I can laugh at! What about X, or Z! Right! Wouldn't that be funny!"

# 47

# MISS SCALPEL

Just as I was reaching the edge of the city outskirts, under flashing gaslights, I felt an arm slipping gently under mine, and I heard a voice speaking in my ear: "Sir, are you a doctor?"

I looked. She was a tall girl, sturdy, with very sincere eyes, light makeup, her hair flowing in the wind with the strings of her bonnet.

"No. I'm not a doctor. Let me go."

"Oh yes! You are a doctor. You really look it. Come to my place. You'll be quite satisfied with me, come on!"

"Sure, I'll come see you, but later, *after the doctor*, what the hell!... "

"Ah! Ah!" she replied, still hanging onto my arm, and bursting out laughing, "you're a jesting doctor. I've known many of that type. Come along."

I passionately love mystery, because I always hope to un-tangle it. So I allowed myself to be dragged off by that com-panion, or rather by that unhoped-for enigma.

I omit the description of her hovel; it can be found in several well-known old French poets. Except, and Régnier did not notice this detail, two or three portraits of famous doctors were hanging on the walls.

How coddled I was! Large fire, warm wine, cigars; and while she served me these good things and lit a cigar for herself, the comical creature told me, "Make yourself at home, my friend, get comfortable. It'll bring back the hospi-tal and the good times of youth. —Ah there! now where did that white hair come from? You weren't like that, not too long ago, when you were an intern under doctor L——. I remember that you were the one who helped him with the major operations. Now there's a man who loves to cut, hack, and saw! You were the one who handed him the instruments, the sutures, and the sponges. —And when the operation was finished, how he would say proudly, checking his watch, 'Five minutes, gentlemen!' —Oh! as for me, I get around. I really know those Gentlemen."

A few moments later, addressing me by the familiar *tu*, she repeated her antiphon, and said, "You are a doctor, aren't you, my kitten?"

That unintelligible refrain made me leap to my feet. Furious I yelled, "No!"

"Surgeon, then?"

"No! no! unless it would be to cut off your head! You damned holy ciborium of Saint Mackeral!"

"Wait," she replied, "you'll see."

And she took a bundle of papers from her cupboard, which was none other than a collection of portraits of famous doctors of the time, lithographed by Maurin, which for several years you could find displayed along the Quai Voltaire.

"Look! Do you recognize that one?"

"Yes! That's X. Anyway his name is at the bottom. But I know him personally."

"I knew you did! Look! Here's Z, the one who told his class, referring to X, 'That monster who carries his soul's darkness on his face!' All that, because the other one didn't agree with his position on the issue! They really joked about that at the Medical School, those days! Don't you remember? —Look, here's K——, the one who denounced to the government the insurgents he was treating at his hospital. That was the period of insurrections. How could such a handsome man have so little heart? —Now here's W——, a famous English doctor; I captured him during his trip to Paris. He looks like a young lady, don't you think?"

And as I was touching a tied-up stack, also lying on the

table, she said, "Wait a bit, that's the interns, and this stack, that's the externs."

And like a fan she spread out a load of photographic pictures, depicting much younger physiognomies.

"When we meet again, you'll give me your portrait, won't you, darling?"

"But," I replied, in turn following, me as well, my obsession, "why do you believe I'm a doctor?"

"It's because you're so nice and so kind to women!"

"Strange logic!" I said to myself.

"Oh! I'm hardly ever wrong. I've known a good number of them. I like those gentlemen so much, that, although I'm not sick, sometimes I go see them, just to see them. Some of them tell me coldly, 'You're not sick at all!' But some of the others understand me, because I give them hints."

"And when they don't understand you?..."

"Mercy! Since I've bothered them *unnecessarily,* I leave ten francs on the mantelpiece. —They're so good and sweet, those men! —I discovered a little intern at the Pitié hospital, as pretty as an angel, and polite! and he works so hard, the poor boy! His pals told me that he doesn't have any money, because his parents are poor and can't send him anything. That encouraged me. After all, I'm a beautiful enough woman, though not too young. I told him, 'Come see me, come see me often. And with me, don't worry. I don't need money.' But you see, I suggested that to him in many ways. I didn't tell him bluntly; I was so afraid of humiliating him, that dear child! —Well! Would you believe I've a funny craving I don't dare tell him about? —I'd like him to come see me with his instrument case and gown, even with a little blood on it!"

She said that quite candidly, as a sensitive man might tell an actress with whom he might make love, "I want to see you dressed in the costume you wore when you created that famous role."

As for me, persisting stubbornly, I continued, "Can you

remember the time and the situation when this so peculiar passion arose in you?"

With difficulty I made myself understood; finally I succeeded. But then she replied very sadly, and even, as far as I can remember, averting her eyes, "I don't know... I don't remember."

What weirdness you find in big cities, when you know how to walk about and look! Life swarms with innocent monsters. —Lord, my God! You, the Creator, you, the Master; you who made Law and Freedom; you, the sovereign who lets things happen, you, the judge who forgives; you who are abounding in motives and causes, and who have perhaps placed a taste for horror in my mind in order to convert my heart, like a cure at knife point; Lord, have pity, take pity on madmen and madwomen! O Creator! Can *monsters* exist in the eyes of the only One who knows why they exist, how they *were made* and how they might have been able *not to be made?*

# N'IMPORTE OÙ HORS DU MONDE
## Any Where Out of the World

This life is a hospital in which every patient is haunted by the desire to change beds. This one wants to suffer in front of the stove, and that one believes he will recover next to the window.

It seems that I would always be content where I am not, and I constantly discuss that question of relocation with my soul.

"Tell me, my soul, poor benumbed soul, what would you think about residing in Lisbon? It must be warm there, and there you would perk up like a lizard. That city is next to the water; they say it is built of marble, and its populace hates vegetation so much that they rip out all the trees. Now there's a landscape to your liking; a landscape made of light and mineral, and of liquid to reflect them!"

My soul does not answer.

"Since you love calm so much, added to the view of movement, do you want to come reside in Holland, that beatifying land? Perhaps that region whose image you have often admired in museums would divert you. What would you say to Rotterdam, you who love forests of masts, and ships moored at the doorsteps of houses?"

My soul remains mute.

"Batavia would appeal to you more? Besides there we would find the spirit of Europe married to tropical beauty."

Not a word. —Might my soul be dead?

"So have you reached that degree of stupor where you can take pleasure only in your affliction? If it is thus, let's flee to-

ward the countries which are the analogies of Death. —I've
just what we need, poor soul! We'll pack our trunks for Tornio. Let's go farther still, to the very edge of the Baltic Sea;
still farther away from life, if that is possible; let's settle at
the pole. There the sun just obliquely grazes the earth's surface, and the slow alternation of light and night abolishes
variety and increases monotony, that one-half of nothingness. There, we can take long baths of darkness, while, to
amuse us, the aurora borealis now and then hurls out its
pink showers, like reflections of fireworks from Hell!"

At last, my soul explodes, and wisely she shouts at me,
"Anywhere! Anywhere! provided it is out of this world!"

# LET'S BEAT UP THE POOR!

For two weeks I had shut myself up in my room, and I had surrounded myself with the books fashionable at that time (sixteen or seventeen years ago); I speak of books dealing with the art of making nations happy, wise, and rich, in twenty-four hours. I had thus digested—swallowed, I mean—all the ramblings of all those managers of public happiness—of those who advise all the poor to become slaves, and those who persuade them that they are all de-throned kings. —It will not be considered surprising that I was then in a state of mind bordering on vertigo or idiocy.

Yet I thought that I sensed, shut deep within my intellect, the dim seed of an idea better than all the old wives' for-mulas I had recently perused in the encyclopedia. But it was only the idea of an idea, something infinitely hazy.

Then I went out quite thirsty. For a passionate craving for shoddy books begets a proportional need for the open air and refreshments.

As I was about to enter a tavern, a beggar held out his hat, with one of those unforgettable looks that would topple thrones, if mind could move matter, and if a hypnotist's eyes could ripen grapes.

At the same time, I heard a voice whispering in my ear, a voice I knew well; the voice of a good Angel, or of a good Demon, who accompanies me everywhere. Since Socrates had his good Demon, why shouldn't I have my good Angel, why shouldn't I have the honor, like Socrates, of acquiring my certificate of insanity, signed by the insightful Lélut and the sagacious Baillarger?

The difference between the Demon of Socrates and my own is that his would appear to him only to forbid, warn, suggest, persuade. That poor Socrates had only a prohibitive demon; mine is a great approver, mine is a Demon of action, or Demon of combat.

This is what its voice whispered to me: "He alone is equal to another, if he proves it, and he alone is worthy of freedom, if he can conquer it."

Immediately, I pounced on my beggar. With a single punch, I shut one eye, which became, in a second, as big as a ball. I broke one of my nails smashing two of his teeth, and since I didn't feel strong enough to beat up the old man quickly, having been born fragile and not well trained in boxing, with one hand I grabbed him by the collar of his outfit, and I gripped his throat with the other, and I began vigorously to bounce his head against a wall. I should admit that beforehand I had examined the surroundings with a glance, and I had ascertained that in that deserted suburb, for a long enough time, I was beyond the reach of any policeman.

Having next, with a kick directed to his back, forceful enough to break his shoulder blades, floored that weakened sexagenarian, I grabbed a big tree branch lying on the ground, and I beat him with the obstinate energy of cooks trying to tenderize a beefsteak.

Suddenly,—Oh miracle! Oh delight of the philosopher who verifies the excellence of his theory!—I saw that antique carcass turn over, straighten up with a force I would never have suspected in a machine so peculiarly unhinged. And, with a look of hatred that seemed to me *a good omen,* the decrepit bandit flung himself on me, blackened both my eyes, broke four of my teeth, and, with the same tree branch beat me to a pulp. —By my forceful medication, I had thus restored his pride and his life.

Then, I made a mighty number of signs to make him understand that I considered the debate settled, and getting up with the self-satisfaction of a Stoic sophist, I told him, "Sir, *you are my equal!* Please do me the honor of sharing my purse. And remember, if you are a true philanthropist, you must apply to all your colleagues, when they seek alms, the theory I had the *pain* to test upon your back."

He indeed swore that he had understood my theory, and that he would comply with my advice.

# THE GOOD DOGS

*To M. Joseph Stevens*


I have never been ashamed of my admiration for Buffon, even in the presence of my century's young writers. But today I will not appeal to the soul of that painter of pompous nature to help me. No.

Much more gladly I would call upon Sterne, and I would say, "Descend from heaven, or ascend to me from the Elysian fields, to inspire me on behalf of good dogs, pitiful dogs, with a song worthy of you, sentimental humorist, incomparable humorist! Return to us riding the famous ass which still accompanies you in posterity's memory; and especially, don't let the ass forget to bring, delicately hanging between its lips, its immortal macaroon!"

Academic muse get away! I don't need that old prude. I invoke the familiar muse, the city muse, the lively muse, so that she will help me sing of good dogs, pitiful dogs, muddied dogs, those everyone shuns, as striken with plague and vermin, except the pauper whose colleagues they are, and the poet, who considers them with a fraternal eye.

Shame on foppish dogs, those conceited quadrupeds, Great Dane, King-Charles spaniel, pug or lap dog, so enchanted with themselves, and so sure to please, that they leap indiscreetly onto the legs or knees of visitors, unruly like children, stupid like easy women, sometimes sulky and insolent like servants! Shame above all on those four-footed serpents, trembling and idle, called greyhounds, and which do not accommodate enough flair in their pointed muzzles to follow a friend's trail, nor enough intelligence in their flat heads to play dominos!

To their dens, all those tedious parasites!

Back to their silky and padded dens! I sing of the mud-died dog, the poor dog, the homeless dog, the stroller dog, the acrobat dog, the dog whose instinct, like that of the poor, of gypsies and actors, is marvelously goaded by necessity, such a good mother, true patroness of minds!

I sing of catastrophic dogs, of those who wander, alone, in the sinuous ravines of huge cities, and of those who tell abandoned people, with winks and witty eyes, "Take me along, and out of our two miseries perhaps we'll create a kind of happiness!"

"*Where do dogs go?*" once wrote Nestor Roqueplan in an immortal story he has probably forgotten, and which I alone, and perhaps Sainte-Beuve, still remember today.

Where do dogs go? You ask, you unmindful people. They go about their business.

Business meetings, love meetings. Through fog, through snow, through mud, during biting dog-days, in streaming rain, they go, they come, they trot, they slip under carriages, urged on by fleas, passion, need, or duty. Like us, they got up early in the morning, and they seek their livelihood or pursue their pleasures.

Some of them sleep in a ruins at the city outskirts and, every day, come at set times, to call for their largess at the door of a Palais-Royal kitchen. Others rush about in packs for more than five leagues, to share a meal prepared for them through the charity of certain sexagenarian maidens, whose deserted hearts are devoted to beasts because stupid men no longer want them.

Others, like runaway Negro slaves, crazed with love, leave their county, on certain days, to visit the city, for an hour, to frisk around a fine bitch, groomed a bit sloppily, but proud and grateful.

And they are all quite punctual, without appointment books, without notes, and without wallets.

Are you acquainted with lazy Belgium, and have you, as I have, marveled at all those energetic dogs harnassed to a butcher's cart, a milkman's, or a baker's, and whose triumphal barking bears witness to the haughty pleasure they feel in competing with horses?

Here are two who belong to an even more civilized order! Allow me to usher you into the room of an absent acrobat. A bed, of painted wood, without curtains, blankets lying about and soiled by bedbugs, two straw chairs, a cast-iron stove, one or two broken musical instruments. Oh, what dreary furniture! But, if you please, look at those two intelligent characters, dressed in clothes both tattered and sumptuous, wearing hats like troubadours or soldiers, who, with a magician's concentration, are supervising *the nameless work* simmering on the lit stove, and at whose center stands a long spoon, planted like one of those aerial masts announcing that the freemasonry is completed.

Don't you think it fair that such zealous actors take to the road only after loading down their stomachs with powerful and solid soup? And will you not grant a little sensuality to those poor devils who all day have to confront the public's indifference and the unfairness of a director who takes the largest share and who alone eats more soup than four actors?

How often have I contemplated, smiling and moved, all those four-footed philosophers, obliging slaves, submissive or devoted, that the republican dictionary could just as well qualify as *public benefactors,* if the republic, too absorbed with the *happiness* of people, had time to care for the *honor* of dogs!

And how often have I thought that perhaps somewhere (who knows, after all?), to reward so much courage, so much patience and toil, there was a special paradise for good dogs, pitiful dogs, muddied and afflicted dogs. Swedenborg indeed maintains that there is one for Turks and one for the Dutch!

— 127 —

The shepherds of Virgil and Theocritus would expect, as payment for their alternating chants, a fine cheese, a flute made by the best, or a goat with swollen udders.

The poet who has sung of pitiful dogs has received as reward a beautiful vest, whose color, both rich and faded, provokes thoughts of autumn suns, of the beauty of mature women and of Indian summers.

None of those present in the tavern on the Villa-Hermosa will forget how impetuously the painter shed his vest on behalf of the poet, so keenly did he recognize how good and honorable it was to sing of pitiful dogs.

Likewise, a magnificent Italian tyrant, of the good old days, would give the divine Aretino a dagger embellished with gems, or a court cloak, in exchange for a precious sonnet or a curious satirical poem.

And every time the poet dons the painter's vest, he is compelled to think of good dogs, of philosophical dogs, of Indian summers, and of the beauty of women quite mature.

# APPENDIX
## Preface to *La Presse*, 1862

To Arsène Houssaye

My dear friend, I send you this little work of which it cannot be said, without injustice, that it has neither head nor tail, since, on the contrary, everything in it is both tail and head, alternatively and reciprocally. Consider, I beg you, what admirable convenience that combination offers us all, you, me, and the reader. We can cut wherever we want, I my reverie, you the manuscript, the reader his reading; for I do not bind the latter's recalcitrant will to the endless thread of a superfluous plot. Remove one vertebra, and the two pieces of that tortuous fantasy will reunite without difficulty. Chop it up into many fragments, and you will find that each one can exist separately. In the hope that some of those segments will be lively enough to please and to divert you, I dare dedicate to you the entire serpent.

I have a little confession to make. It is while perusing, for at least the twentieth time, the famous *Gaspard de la nuit* of Aloysius Bertrand (a book known to you, to me, and to some of our friends, does it not have every right to be called *famous?*), that the idea came to me to try something similar, and to apply to the description of modern life, or rather of *one* modern and more abstract life, the procedure he had applied to the depiction of ancient life, so strangely picturesque.

Which of us has not, in his ambitious days, dreamed of the miracle of a poetic prose, musical without rhythm and without rhyme, supple enough and choppy enough to fit the soul's lyrical movements, the undulations of reverie, the jolts of consciousness?

This obsessive ideal came to life above all by frequenting enormous cities, in the intersection of their countless relationships. You yourself, my dear friend, did you not try to translate the *Glazier*'s strident cry into a *song*, and to express in lyrical prose all the woeful associations that cry sends all the way up to attics, through the street's thickest fogs?

But, truth to tell, I fear that my jealousy has not brought me luck. As soon as I had begun the labor, I noticed that not only did I remain quite far from my mysterious and brilliant model, but more so that I was making something (if that can be called *some thing*) peculiarly different, an accident of which anyone other than I would probably be proud, but which can only deeply humiliate a mind that considers as the poet's greatest honor to execute *exactly* what he planned to do.

Yours most affectionately,
C.B.

# NOTES

Baudelaire's works inevitably provide evidence for current theories of literature and culture. For the first integral interpretation see Edward K. Kaplan, *Baudelaire's Prose Poems: The Esthetic, the Ethical, and the Religious in "The Parisian Prowler"* (Athens: University of Georgia Press, 1990), with its bibliography. Here, as a convenience, are some references readily recognizable in the author's time.

## INTRODUCTION

My notion of Baudelaire's "second revolution" modifies Barbara Johnson's interpretation in *Défigurations du langage poétique* (Paris, 1979). Alicia Borinsky introduced me to the term "theoretical fable" in a lecture at Brandeis University.

*Constantin Guys* (1805–92). An artist whose sketches of contemporary life in London and Paris Baudelaire considered exemplary of a "painter of modern life." My quotation is from Baudelaire, *The Painter of Modern Life and Other Essays*, translated by Jonathan Mayne (London and New York, 1965).

*Georges Blin*'s expression "un commencement absolu" appears in his introduction to the prose poems, in *Le Sadisme de Baudelaire* (Paris, 1948).

*Louis "Aloysius" Bertrand* (1807–41). Author of *Gaspard de la nuit* (posthumously published in 1842), fantasies with often grotesque imagery, inspired by Callot and Rembrandt (see Appendix).

*Arsène Houssaye* (1814–96). A productive, superficial journalist and author of novels and prose poems, who, during 1861–62, was artistic director of the newspaper *La Presse*, which published Baudelaire's most extensive sequence of prose poems (see Appendix).

## 5. THE DOUBLE ROOM

The *Sylphid* appears in the *Mémoires d'outre-tombe* of François-René de Chateaubriand (1768–1848), whose best-selling novella *René* (1802) defined the French romantic anguished adolescent hero to whom Baudelaire refers obliquely as the "little René."

*Laudanum* includes any number of mixtures containing opium, widely used in the nineteenth century as medicine.

The untranslatable French word *ennui*, usually rendered as "boredom," refers to a pathological deadening of the will to live, experienced as clinical depression or suicidal apathy.

## 9. THE BAD GLAZIER

*Minos, Aeacus,* and *Rhadamanthus*. In Greek mythology, the three judges of Hell.

## 11. THE WILD WOMAN AND THE AFFECTED COQUETTE

The quotation at the end alludes to the fable of *Jean de La Fontaine* (1621–95), "The Frogs Who Asked for a King."

## 13. WIDOWS

*Luc de Clapier, marquis de Vauvenargues* (1715–47). Author of the widely read *Maximes*, which present an optimistic view of human nature and passions.

## 14. THE OLD ACROBAT

*Jean-Baptiste Poquelin (Molière,* 1622–73). The great comic playwright and actor of Louis XIV's court.

## 18. INVITATION TO THE VOYAGE

Baudelaire compares his own poem, "L'Invitation au voyage" (*Fleurs du Mal,* no. 53), to "Invitation to the Waltz" by Karl Maria von Weber (1786–1826), considered to be the prototypical romantic composer.

## 20. THE FAIRIES' GIFTS

Baudelaire heaps together *Fairies*, supernatural beings of medieval invention, with *Gnomes* (earth spirits), *Salamanders* (fire spirits), *Sylphids* and *Sylphs* (spirits of the air), and *Nixies* (German for *Undines*, or water sprites).

## 21. THE TEMPTATIONS, OR EROS, PLUTUS, AND FAME

In Greek mythology, *Eros*, the son of Aphrodite, represents desire; *Plutus*, the god of wealth. *Bacchus*, the Roman name for Dionysos, god of wine, is usually represented resting with grapes or cup in hand.

## 23. SOLITUDE

The widely read novel by Daniel Defoe (1660?–1731), depicts the adventures of *Robinson Crusoe*, stranded on an island.

*Antoine-Joseph Santerre* (1752–1809), a commandant of the National Guard during the 1789 Revolution, is reputed to have ordered a rolling of the drums to drown out the last words of Louis XVI before he was executed.

*Jean de La Bruyère* (1645–96). Author of *Les Caractères*, pessimistic portraits of courtiers and other social types of the royal court.

*Blaise Pascal* (1623–62). Author of the *Pensées* (1670), an apology for Jansenism, a morally rigorous approach to Catholicism, which analyzes human motivations in light of spiritual values.

## 25. BEAUTIFUL DOROTHY

The *Kaffirs* are black people of southern Africa; from the Arabic word *kafir*, "infidel."

## 26. THE EYES OF THE POOR

*Ganymede*. A very handsome Trojan prince, abducted by Zeus and made cupbearer of the gods, replacing *Hebe*, daughter of Zeus and goddess of youth.

## 27. A HEROIC DEATH

*Fanciullo* is an Italian word for boy.

*Nero.* Emperor of Rome (54–68 A.D.) and patron of the arts, known for his cruelty and passion for self-advertisement.

## 30. THE ROPE

*Edouard Manet* (1832–83). Outstanding pre-Impressionist painter who became close to Baudelaire after 1863.

## 32. THE THYRSUS

*Franz Liszt* (1811–86). Famous writer, composer, and piano virtuoso whose book on Richard Wagner's opera *Lohengrin* deeply influenced Baudelaire's thoughts on music.

*Bacchant.* Priestess of Bacchus, god of wine.

*Gambrinus,* or Cambrinus. A German king, reputed inventor of beer.

## 36. THE DESIRE TO PAINT

*Witches of Thessaly.* A reference to Book 6 of the historical epic *Pharsalia* by the Roman poet Lucan (A.D. 39–65).

## 37. THE MOON'S BENEFITS.

There is no agreement about the identity of "Mademoiselle B——."

## 42. PORTRAITS OF MISTRESSES

*Cherubino.* A young man in Beaumarchais's play *The Marriage of Figaro* (1784), who represents a type of adolescent just awakening to love.

*Dryads.* Tree nymphs in Greek and Roman mythology.

*Minerva.* The Roman goddess of wisdom and of arts and trades.

## 45. THE SHOOTING RANGE AND THE CEMETERY

*Horace* (65–8 B.C.). A Latin poet who sang of life's pleasures, stressing the moderation of desires and known as a disciple of the

Greek *Epicurus* (341–270 B.C.), vaguely interpreted as a philosopher of facile hedonism (rather, Epicurus preached asceticism).

## 47. MISS SCALPEL

*Maturin Régnier* (1573–1613). A satiric and realistic poet, a dissident who prepared the way for Molière.

*Antoine Maurin* (1799–1850). An artist and engraver, now forgotten; a student of Ary Scheffer.

## 48. ANY WHERE OUT OF THE WORLD

The English title, deliberately misspelled by Baudelaire, reinforces its exotic message.

*Tornio*. A port in Finland on the Swedish frontier.

## 49. LET'S BEAT UP THE POOR!

The Greek philosopher *Socrates* (469–399 B.C.) made enemies in Athens by refuting sophists who paraded their wisdom. His "demon," or *daimon*, refers to the little god attending each person.

*Lélut* and *Baillarger*. Two famous nineteenth-century alienists or psychiatrists. *Dr. Louis-Francisque Lélut* wrote a book (1836, reprinted 1856) demonstrating the insanity of Socrates, Tasso, Pascal, Rousseau, and Swedenborg, among others.

Baudelaire's *"Stoic sophist"* combines Zeno of Elea (c. 450 B.C.), a disciple of Parmenides and a Socrates-like "sophist" who founded dialectics, and Zeno of Citium (end of fourth century B.C.), the founder of Stoicism, who taught under the Painted Portico (or *Stoa Poikile*) in Athens. The Stoics taught that happiness consists in liberation from passions and appetites.

## 50. THE GOOD DOGS

The animal painter *Joseph Stevens* (1816–92) and his brothers, the portrait and genre painter Alfred (1823–1906), and the art dealer Arthur (1825–90), befriended the ailing Baudelaire during his final years in Brussels, Belgium.

The author of a monumental descriptive zoology, *Natural His-*

*tory* (1749–1804, 44 vols.), *Louis-Georges Leclerc, comte de Buffon* (1707–88), provided a superlative model of classical prose.

*Laurence Sterne* (1713–68) wrote the whimsical English novel *Life and Opinions of Tristram Shandy*, in which a donkey eats macaroons.

A "true Parisian," *Nestor Roqueplan* (1804–70) directed the newspaper *Figaro* during the Restoration and administered theaters during the July Monarchy. His drama reviews and stories were serialized in the newspapers *Le Constitutionnel* and *La Presse*.

*Charles-Augustin Sainte-Beuve* (1804–69), poet and novelist, was the most influential literary critic of Baudelaire's time.

*Emmanuel Swedenborg* (1688–1772), Swedish scientist and mystic, claimed to have conversations with angels and demons. His theory of *correspondences*, or living links between the natural and spiritual worlds, influenced romantic writers the world over.

*Virgil* (70–19 B.C.). A great Latin poet, author of *Bucolics*, *Georgics*, and *The Aeneid*, the epic of the founding of the Roman Empire.

*Theocritus* (third century B.C.), a Greek poet of the Alexandrine period imitated by Virgil, represents bucolic and pastoral poetry.

The Prince of Wales Tavern, on the *Villa-Hermosa*, a street in Brussels, was a favorite gathering place for Belgian and French artists.

The Italian court poet *Pietro Aretino* (1492–1556), known ironically as "the divine," terrorized the powerful with his scandalous and licentious satires.

# ILLUSTRATION CREDITS

Frontispiece: Etienne Carjat, *Baudelaire at the Etchings*, photograph, ca. 1860; Giraudon, Paris.

Page xiv: Édouard Manet, *The Philosopher*, etching, 1865–66; Fogg Art Museum, Harvard University, Cambridge, Mass., purchase from the Horace M. Swopp Fund.

Page 2: James McNeill Whistler, *La Mère Gérard*, etching; Boston Public Library, Print Division.

Page 24: James McNeill Whistler, *Finette*, dry point, 1859; S. P. Avery Collection, Miriam & Ira D. Wallach Division of Art, Prints and Photographs, The New York Public Library, Astor, Lenox and Tilden Foundations.

Page 28: Honoré Daumier, *The Saltimbanques Changing Place*, chalk, watercolor, ca. 1865; Wadsworth Atheneum, Hartford, Conn., Ella Gallup and Mary Catlin Sumner Collection.

Page 36: James McNeill Whistler, *Rotherhithe*, etching; Boston Public Library, Print Division.

Page 46: Eugène Delacroix, *Faust Seducing Marguerite*, lithograph, 1828; Fogg Art Museum, Harvard University, gift in memory of Frederick B. Deknatel.

Page 54: Honoré Daumier, *Connoisseurs—Les Amateurs de peinture*, watercolor, charcoal, and pen, ca. 1862–64; Cleveland Museum of Art, Dudley P. Allen Fund, 27.208.

Page 58: Baudelaire, Sketch of Jeanne Duval; Godoy Collection, W. T. Bandy Centre d'Etudes Baudelairiennes, Vanderbilt University.

Page 62: Jacques Callot, *Pantalone, or Cassandro*, etching, 1618–20; Fogg Art Museum, Harvard University, purchase from the Francis Calley Gray Engravings Fund, by exchange.

Page 68: Sketch by Baudelaire, W. T. Bandy Centre d'Etudes Baudelairiennes, Vanderbilt University.

Page 72: Eugène Delacroix, *Mephisto Flying Over a City*, lithograph; Frank Anderson Trapp, Amherst, Mass.

Page 76: Édouard Manet, *Child Carrying a Tray*, etching and aquatint, 1861; Fogg Art Museum, Harvard University, purchase from the Alpheus Hyatt Fund.

Page 82: Édouard Manet, *Le Chanteur Espagnol*, etching; Boston Public Library, Print Division.

Page 88: Édouard Manet, *The Absinthe Drinker*, etching, 1861–62; Fogg Art Museum, Harvard University, loan from the collection of Edouard Sandoz.

Page 92: James McNeill Whistler, *La Vieille aux loques*, etching; Boston Public Library, Print Division.

Page 100: Honoré Daumier, *Actor Posing in Front of a Mirror*, pen and ink, crayon, and watercolor; © 1996 Board of Trustees, National Gallery of Art, Washington, D. C., Rosenwald Collection.

Page 104: Constantin Guys, *Two Gentlemen and a Lady*, pen and ink and watercolor; Fogg Art Museum, Harvard University, gift from the collection of Ian Woodner.

Page 114: Constantin Guys, *A Lady of Fashion*, brown ink and blue, brown, and gray washes over graphite on cream wove paper; Fogg Art Museum, Harvard University, bequest of Collection of Maurice Wertheim, Class of 1906.

Page 124: Félix Bracquemond, *Le Repos*, etching from a painting by Joseph Stevens, S. P. Avery Collection, Miriam & Ira D. Wallach Division of Art, Prints and Photographs, The New York Public Library, Astor, Lenox and Tilden Foundations.

End of book: Charles Méryon, *Le Stryge*, etching; Boston Public Library, Print Division.